Kevin De Bruyne: The Inspiring Story of One of Soccer's Star Midfielders

An Unauthorized Biography

By: Clayton Geoffreys

Visit my website at www.claytongeoffreys.com
Cover photo by Эдгар Брещанов is licensed under CC BY-SA 3.0 / modified from original

Table of Contents

Foreword

Kevin De Bruyne, a Belgian professional footballer, is widely considered one of the world's best. He currently captains both Manchester City and the Belgian national team. Before playing with Manchester City, De Bruyne honed his skills with Genk. He then played for Chelsea, Werder Bremen (on loan), and Wolfsburg, before ultimately finding his home with Manchester City.

Among De Bruyne's impressive list of achievements and awards with Manchester City are multiple Premier League titles and League Cups and FA Cups. His other accolades include PFA Players' Player of the Year, Premier League Playmaker of the Season, UEFA Champions League Squad of the Season, and Manchester City's Player of the Year awards on multiple occasions. Additionally, he was named Bundesliga Player of the Year during his time at Wolfsburg. De Bruyne was also instrumental in the Belgian national team's historic third-place finish at the 2018 FIFA World Cup. Thank you for purchasing *Kevin De Bruyne: The Inspiring Story of One of Soccer's Star Midfielders*. In this unauthorized biography, we will learn Kevin De Bruyne's incredible life story and impact on the game of soccer. Hope you enjoy and if you do, please do not forget to leave a review!

Also, check out my website to join my exclusive list where I let you know about my latest books. To thank you for your purchase, I'll gift you free copies of some of my other books at **claytongeoffreys.com/goodies**.

Or, if you don't like typing, scan the QR code here to go there directly.

Cheers,

Clayton Geoffreys

Visit me at www.claytongeoffreys.com

Introduction

Kevin De Bruyne is one of the most recognized, well-decorated, and revered footballers in world football/soccer today. Famed for his success as a midfielder, he has long been part of the ultra-successful Manchester City team and has collected multiple trophies throughout his career. He serves as the captain for the Premier League and the Belgian national teams for whom he has played over 100 times. De Bruyne's success has led to him being labeled a "complete footballer," as he has numerous skills on and off the ball.[i] In the wake of Manchester City's remarkable treble-winning season, pundits have applauded the Belgian as the team's most important component and marveled at his longevity at the club. Some have even called him the greatest midfielder in the game.[ii]

Early Life

Kevin De Bruyne was born on June 28, 1991, in the Belgian village of Drongen.[iii] As a child, Kevin was known to be exceptionally shy.[iv] As such, he found it difficult to make friends as a youngster.[v] He was known to be more than just quiet, however. He also achieved good grades in school, excelled at football, and started almost no trouble. A model student, Kevin even made national Belgian news as one of the few students who benefitted from a scheme at his school where 100% punctual attendance was rewarded with a football match ticket![vi]

While Kevin De Bruyne sees himself as a proud Belgian, his family roots are spread out across a few destinations. His mother, Anna, and father, Herwig, moved the family around Belgium, the UK, and even parts of Africa. His father was a major investor in the oil trade, which often necessitated travel,[vii] meaning that Kevin was exposed to multiple cultures during his upbringing.

Long after his career took off, De Bruyne revealed that he had idolized Michael Owen as a child and tried to emulate his forward play.[viii] As such, he has since admitted that, while growing up, he watched and supported Liverpool, as he would watch football with his grandfather, who was an ardent Liverpool fan.[ix] He might have even tried to emulate the former Liverpool and Manchester United striker on the fields of Drongen. Furthermore, it was clear that Kevin not only loved soccer but he also demonstrated a natural aptitude for the game, practically from the time he learned to walk! De Bruyne began playing soccer at the tender age of four.

While playing with his friends, his talent was obvious, as he was a cut above his peers even during those early years. He has since shared an amusing anecdote involving a particular friend's garden, where they would sometimes play, but Kevin was only allowed to shoot with his left foot, which was his weaker foot at the time. This rule was implemented by the mother of his friend, but not to help Kevin develop more skill with his left foot. Instead, it was because his friend's mother said that his already-powerful right foot was destroying too many plants in the garden![x]

After a few years of playing with his local Drongen team, Kevin was spotted by the KAA Gent scouting team and joined their youth academy, then moved on to Genk in 2005.[xi] This meant leaving his family home and living on the other side of Belgium with a foster family when he was only 15 years old.

After the first season, a problem arose, as the family who took care of Kevin decided that they did not want to have him back. His mother Anna relayed the conversation she had with them over the phone. "They said you're too quiet. They can't interact with you. They said you were difficult."[xii]

De Bruyne was blindsided by this revelation. He had been doing well in school, progressing nicely on the football field, and had not been fighting with anyone, including his foster family. So, to hear that his foster family had perceived his inherent shyness as being "difficult" was not only a shock but also a disappointment.

But rather than being deterred by that turn of events, Kevin used that disappointment to fuel his efforts in his career, making him more determined than ever to become a great success on the pitch. And his efforts paid off. As soon as 2009, he found himself training with Genk's first team. Kevin has since stated that the foster family once spoke to him after a match to express that there was a misunderstanding, however, at the time, he did not accept their apology—and who could blame him? But, in retrospect, perhaps they had done him a favor in disguise!

As a result of the foster family's rejection, Kevin had to join a local boarding school in the area. There, he lived with another emerging talent, Steven Defour. Defour has often remarked about his time living with De Bruyne, saying that his commitment and talent were always evident.

"He knew he wanted to be a professional player. You could see when you were talking to him. He just wanted to play football and prove it," Defour said. "He was quiet, a good guy, who wanted to play football … We were always playing on the PlayStation or football outside … Even then, he could see things way faster than anyone else, so he could argue with the coach … Not really arguing, but if the coach said, 'You have to play the ball right,' he would say no if he could see a better option, because he was so ahead of his teammates."[xiii]

Chapter 1: Club Career

2008-09: First Two Senior Appearances

In May 2009, Genk had one distinct mission for the season—win the Croky Cup. The team had not been competitive in the league that year and was set for a mid-table finish at best. This led the team's caretaker manager, Pierre Denier, to shuffle his team for the late league games, as those remaining games were essentially *dead rubbers*. (This meant that the games were essentially meaningless to the team's outcome at that point. You often see this with American football as well, as NFL teams that no longer have a chance to make the playoffs will often give their starters a rest and play more of their bench players.)

Thus, Kevin De Bruyne played his first minutes of professional football in this setting, as he was brought on for the dying embers of the last two league matches of the season, both of which were losing affairs. De Bruyne was then named on the bench for the Croky Cup final but was not used in the game. Despite this, he still celebrated with the team when Genk recorded a 2-0 win against Mechelen. Winning a trophy in his first-ever professional season would set the tone for the rest of his career.

2009-10: Breaking into the First Team at KAA Genk

De Bruyne was seen as a useful rotation option by the newly appointed Genk manager, Hein Vanhaezebrouck, who began to bring him on or off during games. The early season saw Genk play in UEFA Europa League qualifying games and multiple domestic competitions. However, with the season advancing, De Bruyne's playing time was severely reduced to the point where he was merely making cameo, three-minute appearances in matches. There was a direct correlation between his lack of involvement and the overall results of Genk, with the team losing multiple games.

With the losses piling up, Vanhaezebrouck was eventually dismissed in late November 2008. The next managerial appointment at Genk proved to be one of the most important in Kevin De Bruyne's career. Franky Vercauteren recognized his potential and started to involve him a lot more. During this run, Kevin scored his first professional goal, a thrilling, long-range effort against Standard Liege that proved to be the winning goal.

This resulted in De Bruyne's starting all four of the post-season playoff games for European qualification, scoring one and assisting two goals in the 5-2 aggregate win against Antwerp's Westerlo. It was a long season for the youngster, as he made 40 appearances across all competitions in this debut campaign.

2010-11: Silverware with Genk

Frank Vercauteren continued to show his faith in Kevin De Bruyne by keeping him in the starting line-up at Genk, and he started the 2010-11 season in exceptional form. This included scoring two goals in the 5-0 win against RSC Charleroi and providing assists in three consecutive matches. De Bruyne also scored and assisted in the 5-1 away win against FC Inter Turku, helping Genk win this early UEFA Europa League qualifying tie. However, the team came up short in the next round as it lost 7-2 to FC Porto.

The lack of continental football allowed Genk to focus on their domestic dominance; they went unbeaten in their first 11 games of the league season, winning 9 of the matches. But disaster was around the corner for De Bruyne, as he was hit with a severe case of glandular fever.[xiv] His illness kept him out of action for around two months.

Genk initially struggled without De Bruyne. This was perhaps quite telling, as they suffered their first loss of the season when he wasn't available. This also coincided with Genk exiting the Croky Cup competition without De Bruyne playing.

De Bruyne returned to first-team action when he came off the bench in a league game against Eupen for two minutes at the end of the game. He enjoyed a remarkable outing against KV Kortrijk where he scored and assisted to help the team win 3-2 after they were behind twice in the game. He also went on to assist another three goals as

Genk finished second in the league before the second phase of competition.

Genk relied on exceptional performances from De Bruyne to navigate the remaining 10 games of the season. He had a hand in each of Genk's goals in the 3-2 win against Gent as he scored one and assisted the other two.

Genk won the league title on the last day of the season and De Bruyne earned his first-ever piece of silverware. He was critical to the team winning the title, considering that he played 26 of the league games. This was the first season in which Kevin De Bruyne's creative abilities were fully showcased as he made 17 assists across all competitions.

2011-12: First UEFA Champions League Experience, Signing for Chelsea

Having won the Belgian Pro League in the 2010-11 season, Genk had stamped their ticket for UEFA Champions League football, giving De Bruyne his first experience of the esteemed league. Yet, with the stature of the Belgian league and their coefficient, the team needed to stay in the 2011-12 season early to qualify for the group stage. De Bruyne played in both legs of the tie against Partizan as they progressed to the next round against Maccabi Haifa.

By this point, it was clear that Genk valued De Bruyne immensely and wanted him to play every minute of the campaign. However, another injury was around the corner for the rising soccer phenom, as Kevin seriously hurt his fibula in the second league game against Lierse SK. This injury would cause him to miss around six weeks of action, including the aforementioned qualification tie against Maccabi Haifa.[xv] Fortunately, his teammates were able to win the tie and secure group-stage football after a penalty shoot-out.

The young midfielder was reintroduced to the first team with a substitute appearance against OH Leuven, which ended 1-1 in late September. This proved to be a warm-up, as the team undoubtedly wanted him game-ready for the second match of the UEFA Champions League group stage against Bayer Leverkusen.

De Bruyne played every minute of the next four UCL games—but may have wished he didn't! Genk lost three of them, including a 5-0 dismantling at Stamford Bridge by the hands of Chelsea and a 7-0 embarrassing defeat to Valencia. The 20-year-old Belgian showed his resolve by saying that he wanted to get his own back on Chelsea for the heavy defeat, despite being linked with the club [xvi]

Kevin De Bruyne was now showing that he was cut above the Belgian Pro League as his performances were enough to win games. Nothing better exemplified this point than his hat-trick-scoring game against Club Brugge that ended 5-4 to Genk.[xvii] But Kevin's ambitions were now beginning to outgrow what Genk could offer him, as he wanted to replicate such performances in the UEFA Champions League, but he knew it would be difficult with a Belgian team. During this season, he infamously gave a scathing, half-time interview in which he lambasted some of his teammates, commenting in obvious frustration, "I'm ashamed of them. I suggest that those who don't have a desire to play just leave."[xviii]

By the end of January 2012, it was confirmed that Kevin De Bruyne would become a Chelsea player. The deal did, however, allow Genk to retain his services for the rest of the 2011-12 season, as he would be immediately loaned back to the Belgian club.[xix] While De Bruyne remained committed to the club, the results were not nearly as fruitful as the season prior. He continued to perform on a solo basis, notably making nine direct goal contributions in the last five games of the first phase of the league season.

Genk qualified for the Champions pathway second stage of the league, with De Bruyne assisting almost at will. After four wins from the first five games, Genk even dared to dream of salvaging the season. But that hope was quickly derailed when, 12 minutes into the game against Anderlecht, De Bruyne was forced off the pitch due to injury. Genk would go on to lose the game 4-0 and finish third in the league.

Perhaps more significantly, that injury meant that Kevin De Bruyne had played his last game for Genk before the conclusion of the season. Although his discontent and impending departure from the club was now public knowledge, Kevin remarked at the time that it was not the way he wanted to leave the club. "I didn't think this, no. Not like this, anyway. But I can't turn back the clock."[xx]

His former teammate and captain at Genk, David Hubert, only had praise for De Bruyne. While some of the team thought he was cheeky and rude, Hubert noted, "It was a shock, because this kid was moaning at us, telling us we weren't playing well and demanding we did what he told us! But do you know what? We actually respected him for it. He was right, and we admired he had the confidence to ask for better. The feeling was, come on, let's not let down the young guy ... The more time these senior players spent with De Bruyne, the more they appreciated how high he was setting the bar—how he saw the game in a different way than the rest of them ... He got frustrated as he saw things other players didn't ... He would then give them the solutions and tell them to make certain runs so they were in the right position ... Kevin was not just talk. He was doing it on the pitch. He was speaking with his feet and his mouth. We were soon in awe of him."[xxi]

Throughout the season, De Bruyne was primarily used in two positions, either in the left-midfield role or the central midfield placement. While neither proved to be his most successful position, at this juncture, he was significantly outperforming his Genk teammates as he scored 8 times and made 15 assists across all competitions.

2012-13: Finally Heading to London—Sort Of!

Kevin De Bruyne finally linked up with Chelsea and was included in their pre-season tour of the United States. The Belgian came on in the second half of the game against the Seattle Sounders, a match that

Chelsea won 4-2.[xxii] He also came on in the game against the MLS All-Stars in a losing effort.[xxiii] But, whether or not Chelsea manager Roberto Di Matteo liked what he saw from De Bruyne, the management ultimately decided that the next phase of the young Belgian's career should be away from Stamford Bridge where he could compete for first-team football.[xxiv] This resulted in the 21-year-old being sent to Werder Bremen on a season-long loan.[xxv]

2012-13: Loaned to Werder Bremen

Kevin De Bruyne was immediately put into the starting eleven by Werder Bremen manager Thomas Schaaf. This meant playing in the season-opener against the reigning Bundesliga champions, Borussia Dortmund, a game that ended 2-1 to Dortmund.[xxvi] The young Belgian made his first direct goal contribution in German football in the game against Hannover 96, sadly another game that saw Werder Bremen lose.[xxvii] De Bruyne followed that up with another goal in the following match against VfB Stuttgart as he began to announce himself in the Bundesliga.

While he was first played as a center-forward, Schaaf soon put De Bruyne into an attacking midfield position where he was able to excel by setting up teammates like Marco Arnautovic, Sebastian Prodl, and Nils Petersen with decent regularity. De Bruyne continued to play well, always starting matches and cropping up with assists and goals, but the team was not able to play in his image. This was displayed in the defeats against Bayer Leverkusen, Borussia Dortmund, and

Bayern Munich, all of which Werder Bremen lost by multiple goals. De Bruyne did get the consolation goal against the latter, however, which was a nice personal moment.[xxviii]

By this point, there were some obvious similarities to his time spent at Genk in that he was performing well but the team was continuing to struggle. De Bruyne scored four goals in the last three games of the Bundesliga season, yet Werder Bremen failed to win any of the games. The team finished a dismal fourteenth in the league.

Come the end of the 2012-13 season, there seemed to be some confusion and conjecture about the future of Kevin De Bruyne. Earlier in the season, Kevin commented, "So there was a series of misunderstandings. I never said that I was happy that I only signed for one year in Bremen. I said that I was happy to have signed with Werder because they were giving me a chance to play a lot. I also said that Chelsea remains my employer and that Werder made it clear to me that I can only stay here one year."[xxix]

At this point, Kevin was keeping his options open but ultimately would not tie himself down to a specific destination. Mostly, De Bruyne was simply pleased to have avoided relegation come the end of the season, as the campaign was a slog for everyone involved with the club.

"We've managed this together," he said. "I don't [see myself as any kind of savior.] I played in a more advanced role, so it's up to me to score goals. We're all just happy still to be in the Bundesliga."[xxx]

15

While he was happy to state that it was a team effort to avoid relegation, many pundits have since said that if Werder Bremen did not have the young Belgian for this season, they would not have survived the drop.[xxxi]

Throughout this loan season at Werder Bremen, De Bruyne was asked to perform multiple roles and played various positions across the pitch. The majority of those positions proved to be in the attacking midfield where he was able to excel with creative and offensive moves. In total, he scored 10 Bundesliga goals and notched up 9 assists too. In the season, he played 33 of the 34 league matches.

While some Werder Bremen fans might look back on De Bruyne's exit from Werder Bremen as being a bit unharmonious and ambiguous, Kevin remarked that he enjoyed his time at the club and made solid relationships during the tenure as well.

"For the road games, I share a room with Nils Petersen. I have a good relationship with him. He's a very nice guy … I also get along well with Klaus Allofs. We also laughed together in our talk today and made some jokes."[xix]

He returned to Chelsea for the upcoming summer pondering what his next move would be.

2013-14: Leaving Chelsea for VfL Wolfsburg

Chelsea was now back under the management of Jose Mourinho, the legendary Portuguese manager who had previously taken the South

West London club to the apex of English football. He granted Kevin De Bruyne the chance to play for his spot by taking him on both pre-season tours to Asia and later the U.S. The Belgian would go on to score in games against the Malaysian national team and AC Milan.

Mourinho soon made his decision on the young midfielder, as he was used sparingly in the first few Premier League fixtures and was not selected at all in the UEFA Super Cup squad. After September 2012, De Bruyne was limited to keeping the bench warm and rotated use in the cup competitions.

De Bruyne, at this point, took his career in his own hands. Sensing he still would not get much play time at Stamford Bridge, he stated, "No, I am not going to get the opportunities I need here."[xxxii] He then opted to return to Germany when he joined VfL Wolfsburg on a permanent deal in January 2014.[xxxiii] The transfer fee was reported to be around 20 million euros.[xxxiv]

When asked about his troubled stint and exit from Chelsea, De Bruyne has often been quick to dismiss any irritation or strife he had with the club or Jose Mourinho. "I think they (Chelsea) had a different view than I had of myself. I was young but also experienced. If I had come through the youth then maybe I would be happy to play 10 games there. I think Eden Hazard was the same age as me when he played, so it's a little bit strange to say this guy is young and the other guy is old enough to play ... but I have no problem with Jose."[xxxv]

To date, Chelsea is the only club that De Bruyne has played for but did not score a goal. His lone goal contribution for the London club came on the opening day of the 2013-14 season when he set up Oscar against Hull City.

One week after joining Wolfsburg, De Bruyne was put into the starting eleven to bolster their chances of a good finish in the Bundesliga table and qualify for continental football. He was again starting games at a club that saw him as part of their long-term project. He was assisting goals soon after he arrived, but endured yet another 6-1 defeat at the hands of Bayern Munich. The game against FC Augsburg was a memorable match for De Bruyne, even if for the wrong reasons, as he received two yellow cards in the space of a minute; he was sent off and would miss the following Bundesliga game against his former club, Werder Bremen.

Wolfsburg would end up finishing fifth in the league, but Kevin De Bruyne was in a better place regardless. He was now at a club that valued his abilities and wanted to play with him in the team. This would be the platform for his future successes.

2014-15: Breakout Season in Germany

For many soccer fans, the 2014-15 season was the campaign in which Kevin De Bruyne truly came of age and showed everyone his mettle. Now an established starting member at Volkswagen Arena, De Bruyne would be instrumental in the attacking midfield. The season started with an arbitrary loss to Bayern Munich but after that, the season turned around.

De Bruyne started to produce around an assist per game, allowing Wolfsburg to ascend the Bundesliga standings by defeating teams like Bayer Leverkusen, VfB Stuttgart, and even Werder Bremen. Wolfsburg wanted to push for the Bundesliga title and the 4-1 victory against Bayern Munich in which De Bruyne scored two goals, certainly helped the cause.[xxxvi] This spurred a series of good results and performances for both the team and the player.

Dieter Hecking, the manager of Wolfsburg, wanted De Bruyne to play a part in every game. This meant that the young Belgian was also part of the team's UEFA Europa League squad. While the team lost home and away to Everton, the group stage was fruitful for the German outfit. De Bruyne scored a late equalizer against LOSC Lille, two against Krasnodar away from home, and then assisted two more in the home match against the aforementioned Russian team. These results were enough for Wolfsburg to progress to the knockout phase.

The first tie was against Sporting CP from Portugal, with De Bruyne assisting in the home tie as Wolfsburg won 2-0 on aggregate. The Round of 16 matches against Inter Milan were a showcase of Kevin De Bruyne's skills as an attacking footballer.[xxxvii] His two goals at home and an assist in Italy ensured progression to the next round.[xxxviii] This series of games has been reported to be the match that convinced Manchester City to make him a prime transfer target.[xxxix] However, his heroics would not be enough to help the team overcome SSC Napoli, as Wolfsburg lost 6-3 on aggregate.

Wolfsburg continued to win games in the Bundesliga but not even De Bruyne's excellent performances could help them eclipse Bayern Munich, who finished 10 points ahead of them in the league standings. By the end of this season, speculation was rife as to where De Bruyne would play his football next season.

His former coach at Genk, Pierre Denier, applauded the player and stated that many doors would be open to him, given his exceptional performances in Germany.[xl] By this time, Kevin was attracting a lot of attention as a potential transfer for the elite clubs in Europe.

De Bruyne spoke to Eurosport about the speculation. "What will happen in the summer, I don't know … As a player, it is so stupid to say that I will stay here and then some big club is coming in and offering Wolfsburg a lot of money that they want and they say you can go or something like that. I'm very happy here and I think I will play here next season, but I can't give you a 100% guarantee."[xli]

In the Bundesliga season, De Bruyne played against his former club, Werder Bremen, now decked out in the slightly different green-and-white shade of Wolfsburg. De Bruyne assisted one goal in the 2-1 win at home but was altogether more productive in the away leg on the ground he used to call home. The majority of Werder Bremen fans welcomed De Bruyne back with a warm welcome, as he had been complimentary of the club in the build-up to his return. He put together a hat-trick of assists as Wolfsburg went 5-3 on the night. After the match, he was respectful in his comments. "I am happy. Here's to the return to Bremen, to the Werder Stadium, and to the Werder fans." He later thought that the team was going in the right direction.[xlii]

De Bruyne also played a starring role in the DFB-Pokal campaign as Wolfsburg progressed through the rounds. The Belgian played 120 minutes in the opening round, which needed penalties against Darmstadt 98. After the first round, Wolfsburg continued to win every game with De Bruyne starting them all. This culminated in the team reaching the final against Borussia Dortmund. The young Belgian scored the goal for Wolfsburg to take the lead at 2-1 after 33 minutes of play and the team ultimately won 3-1 on the night. De Bruyne's exceptional play in the game was described as "magical,"[xliii] as he helped the club earn its first piece of silverware in six years.[xliv]

De Bruyne was named Player of the Year in Germany for his remarkable season, which had culminated in 10 goals and 21 assists.[xlv] This assist tally set a new Bundesliga record for the most assists for an individual player in a single season, as De Bruyne continued to immortalize himself in both Wolfsburg and Bundesliga folklore.[xlvi] That record would stand until 2020, when it was finally eclipsed by Thomas Muller.[xlvii]

In addition, he was named the Bundesliga Player of the Season.[xlviii] He also garnered high praise from the club's sporting director, Klaus

Allofs. "That's quite something and there's no reason to talk it down … [He has] the extra class you need to play at the top level."[xlix]

De Bruyne was also elected as the Cup Hero of the 2014-15 season and had his footprints immortalized in the DFB Cup Walk of Fame in front of the Berlin Olympic Stadium.[l] When asked about the season, De Bruyne revealed that he thoroughly enjoyed receiving such praise.

"To be named the best player in a foreign country—that's some going … This is great recognition of my season."[li]

Kevin De Bruyne ended the season having made 51 appearances across all competitions. It was one of his most prolific seasons to date, as he scored 16 goals and assisted a further 28 in both domestic and continental tournaments.

2015-16: Heading to Manchester City

De Bruyne started the season as a VfL Wolfsburg player, however, speculation was high throughout the summer that he would leave the club. The Wolfsburg manager, Dieter Hecking, even lashed out when persistently and repeatedly asked if De Bruyne would be leaving the club.

"It's irritating because the questions don't change and we cannot always change our answers either," Hecking admonished. "I can't be bothered to talk about it anymore. The club has made its position clear … We cannot react to everything ... I don't care and, as a coach, I can't give an update every single day."[lii]

Despite Manchester United initially showing interest stemming back to January 2016,[liii] it was Manchester City who later became the leading party to sign De Bruyne.[liv]

The man who gave Kevin De Bruyne his international debut, Georges Leekens, told *Goal* that he believed the Belgian would only elevate his career at Manchester City. "I think he can go to the highest level … I mean on the Messi, Ronaldo, and Hazard level. He has already shown what he can do."[lv]

At the time of the transfer speculation, De Bruyne's national team manager, Marc Wilmots, was one of the few voices who did not endorse Kevin's potential move to Manchester City. "In my opinion, he should stay at Wolfsburg for one or two more years."[lvi] The Belgian national head coach believed it would be of better benefit for him to continue to develop in the Bundesliga instead of taking a big transfer move.

But for the Wolfsburg coaching staff, it was simply business as normal. De Bruyne was named to the starting eleven for the DFB-Super Cup. He proved to be imperative in that game, as he brilliantly set up Nicklas Bendtner to level the score in the 89th minute. The Belgian also went on to score in the proceeding penalty shootout as the team won another trophy.[lvii] He also scored in the opening round of the 2015-16 DFP-Pokal as well as playing in the first two Bundesliga games of the campaign. However, De Bruyne was granted special leave for the third match to finalize his move to Manchester City.

Kevin De Bruyne was then officially announced as a Manchester City player for over £50m (nearly $63 million U.S.) in transfer fees.[lviii] He made his debut for Manchester City in the fifth Premier League of the season against Crystal Palace at Selhurst Park, a 1-0 win for the Citizens.

The rest of his embryonic phase with Manchester City was a resounding personal success. He scored in the games against West Ham United and Tottenham Hotspur, although the team ultimately lost both games. The subsequent game against Newcastle United proved to be the stimulus for his success at the club, however, as he scored once again and provided two assists in a resounding 6-1 win.

Even with this remarkable performance, De Bruyne thought he could do better. "I'm happy with the second half but I wasn't pleased with the way I played in the first half," he commented. "I found it a bit difficult early on but then you come out again and just try to play better and things came off for me … As for the goal, I didn't hit it perfectly but it went in so it doesn't matter!"[lix]

De Bruyne's spectacular assist for Sergio Aguero has subsequently been named one of his most impressive assists throughout his career as it was driven by unstoppable power from his left foot.

Another key moment in this early phase of De Bruyne's Manchester City career was his leading role in the first Manchester derby of the season as he was pivotal in the 2-1 victory against Manchester United.[lx]

Kevin instantly endeared himself to the fans as he explained the importance of the win. "After the first 15 minutes of the second half we came back stronger and had to change our style a bit because they had a few chances. It was a fight until the end and we're very happy to get the win."

When asked specifically about whether beating Manchester United at Old Trafford was special, Kevin said, "For the fans, yes. For us, it is only three points, but we're happy and the fans will certainly celebrate tonight."[lxi]

Kevin continued to impress in a Manchester City shirt as the team largely won its matches, with De Bruyne putting in memorable performances against Southampton and Sunderland AFC. He also displayed a penchant for the League Cup competition, as he scored four goals in the opening three rounds against tough teams including Sunderland, Crystal Palace, and Hull City. He also assisted in each of those matches. Manchester City won four of its six UEFA Champions League group stage games with De Bruyne scoring against Sevilla in the home match.

By the end of the calendar year, Kevin De Bruyne was named the Belgian Sportsman of the Year for 2015.[lxii] While this accolade was of great importance to De Bruyne, it was little comfort to him when, come the turn of the year, he found himself on the injured list. He had picked up a debilitating knee injury in the second leg of the League Cup semi-final tie against Everton, a game in which he had scored and assisted.[lxiii] The initial scans indicated that he could be out for as many as 10 weeks and potentially miss the European Championships.[lxiv]

Unfortunately, he did miss the League Cup final because of his injury. However, he cheered from the sidelines as Manchester City defeated Liverpool on penalties. The team also lost four out of seven Premier League games while he was unavailable, clearly demonstrating how much his presence was missed on the pitch. The team also exited the FA Cup while their prized Belgian midfielder remained out of action.

By early April 2016, De Bruyne was back in the team and ahead of his recovery schedule.[lxv] This resulted in Manchester City getting back to their winning ways, as De Bruyne even scored a goal on his return. He then scored one more against Arsenal, helping Manchester City secure fourth place in the Premier League table.

Back on the continent, De Bruyne was a driving force in the quarter-final tie, deftly scoring both home and away in the matches against Paris Saint-Germain.[lxvi] His goal in the concluding home leg was one for the record books, as it sparked both quality and importance. The Manchester faithful was on tenterhooks with the aggregate score delicately balanced at 2-2 from the Parisian leg. Then, 76 minutes into the match at Etihad Stadium, the teams were still locked together. That was when Kevin De Bruyne curled an effort from just outside the box beyond three PSG outfield players as well as Kevin Trapp in goal to send the City fans into rapturous cheers.[lxvii] The result stood at 1-0 on the night, and De Bruyne's goal separated the sides to put Manchester City in its first-ever UEFA Champions League semi-final.

De Bruyne and company were unable to replicate the same success against Real Madrid, however, as the team came unstuck and lost 1-0 on aggregate in the semi-final.

It was clear that Kevin De Bruyne had settled perfectly into his new surroundings at Manchester City and made an instant impact at the club. Across the entire season, he played 51 games, scored 15 goals, and set up 17 assists for his teammates. De Bruyne won the League Cup in his first season and, in addition, won the German Super Cup with VfL Wolfsburg before moving to England in the summer transfer window.

2016-17: Continuing to Grow with Manchester City

De Bruyne knew of Pep Guardiola. He had heard about the legendary soccer manager from his time in Germany when he saw Bayern Munich succeed, and while he was still playing for Werder Bremen and VfL Wolfsburg. He was later quoted about his excitement about working with him.

"It's his eye for detail that counts. When he speaks to me, we speak about everything. He was a player himself, so he's very good at knowing the balance of when to joke and when to be serious. Before a game, he'll be really quiet. He does his meetings a couple of hours before the match, and then we are doing stuff on our own. By then, everybody knows what we need to do."[lxviii]

Pep afforded players like Kevin De Bruyne, who had an extended run in the European Championships, more time off than others. Therefore, the Belgian did not feature in any great capacity during the pre-season. De Bruyne did, however, come off the bench during the Super Match exhibition against Arsenal held in Sweden, which the London team won 3-2.[lxix]

The Premier League season started with great excitement for both De Bruyne and the team as he made seven direct goal contributions, helping Manchester City win all of its six opening games in spectacular style. This also included navigating the UEFA Champions League playoff round by soundly defeating Steaua Bucharest 6-0 on aggregate. A minor hamstring injury kept De Bruyne out of the seventh league game against Tottenham and the Champions League group stage match against Celtic.[lxx] But this turned out to be a fairly innocuous knock and he was back in action for the next game.

Now getting used to playing UEFA Champions League football, Manchester City was given a difficult draw against Borussia Monchengladbach, FC Barcelona, and Celtic FC. De Bruyne's most memorable highlight was perhaps scoring a beautiful free-kick against Barcelona.[lxxi] In the post-match interview, he said, "They didn't know how to break us ... I knew that I could get that goal in the corner!"[lxxii] This and the other results were enough to ensure that the team qualified for the knockout stage.

The new year was a good period for the player, as he scored in consecutive matches against Tottenham Hotspur and West Ham United, and City went on to win more than its fair share of games. Pep Guardiola reserved De Bruyne from immediate use in the FA Cup competition, as he wanted to focus on the other competitions. However, the team still made it to the semi-final stage, although they were defeated by Arsenal at this juncture. The other domestic cup competition, the League Cup, ended much more prematurely as De Bruyne sat out the fourth round match against Manchester United with a calf injury and City was eliminated.[lxxiii]

The early exit theme was an unwanted pall surrounding the team, as Manchester City also endured awful luck when they were defeated by Monaco on away goals and the aggregate score finished 6-6. Yet given that Monaco scored three in Manchester, they were cast out of the competition.[lxxiv] This rule has since been abolished, adding extra insult to injury.[lxxv]

With no more competitions left to play for other than the Premier League, Guardiola spent the latter part of the season trying to find the perfect team to help him succeed in the future. Man City would end up finishing third in the table, 15 points behind the eventual winners, Chelsea.

Kevin De Bruyne was deployed in numerous positions throughout the season, commonly entrusted with duties on the left of midfield or the left wing. He would also be put in his trademark central or attacking-midfield position. But, at this juncture, Pep was still perfecting his Manchester City team.

De Bruyne showed more creative efforts as he made 21 assists in all competitions alongside his 7 goals for the season. Unfortunately, the season did not result in any silverware as the team recorded a rare trophyless season. His 18 assists in the Premier League did, however, make him the most fruitful player for assists in the entirety of the season. There was no denying that De Bruyne had become a force to be reckoned with, and he was only getting better.

2017-18: 37 Games in Title-Winning Season

The 2017-18 season started in remarkable fashion for Manchester City. The team won 9 of their opening 10 games in the Premier League, going undefeated in the process. Kevin De Bruyne proved to be integral during this phase as a creative outlet, notably assisting two goals against Liverpool in the 5-0 win at home on match day four. He also showed success in other positions as he scored the winning goal against Chelsea while playing as the right winger.

The Belgian also proved to be just as important in the UEFA Champions League, as he provided a direct goal contribution in the first four games of the group stage, and the team qualified with games to spare.

De Bruyne had a truly remarkable and memorable game against Napoli in the UEFA Champions League, not only for his on-field performance but also for a half-time argument with his teammate, David Silva.[lxxvi]

It was during the game against Feyenoord which City won 4-0 when Pep Guardiola truly came to appreciate the quality of the player he had on the roster in De Bruyne. Following the game, Pep stated that KDB was "one of the best players" he'd ever seen.[lxxvii] After all, this was a game in which he essentially ran the midfield.

Guardiola did not want to exhaust De Bruyne by playing him excessively. Therefore, he rested him for the first match of the League Cup. Pep did, however, turn to the player in the fourth-round match against the Wolverhampton Wanderers as an 82nd-minute substitute. The Belgian was unable to break the deadlock as it stood at 0-0, and the game eventually went to penalties. Thankfully, De Bruyne scored his kick, and City were able to progress despite a little scare!

The team's winning ways continued in the Premier League as Manchester City went on to dispatch teams with apparent ease. De Bruyne went on a scoring rout as he notched up five goals in eight league games—a fantastic return for a player who, at the time, was playing a central midfield role.

City ended the calendar year unbeaten in the league, going from strength to strength. The game and performance against Tottenham Hotspur again left Pep Guardiola almost speechless, as he loved everything he saw from De Bruyne and expressed his desire to build the team around him.

"His performance today, I have no words, no words to describe what he has done with the ball, how many assists, his (ability to) switch play ... The fact that he is one of the most talented players and you see him, how he runs without the ball, he is a good example for the young players, for our academy ... They know how good Kevin De Bruyne is and they can see how he runs and fights without the ball and that is the best example. He helps us to be a better club, a better institution for the future; that is what we want to do."[lxxviii]

At 22 games in, nobody had truly looked like they could stop them— that was, until Liverpool derailed any hopes of the team going invincible when they handed them a narrow 4-3 defeat at Anfield.

While some teams might have been shellshocked at the defeat, Pep Guardiola used it to galvanize his team and, unfazed, they simply started another impressive winning run. De Bruyne managed to provide a hat-trick of assists in the 5-1 defeat of Leicester City as the team bounced back and still sat at the top of the Premier League table.

The semi-final of the League Cup competition was another opportunity for De Bruyne to show his worth. He proudly wore the captain's armband for the first time in the home game against Bristol City and played with the aplomb of a born leader.[lxxix] He led from the front in both legs of the tie as he scored both in Manchester and at Ashton Gate, with Man City winning 5-3 on aggregate.

This set up a final appearance against Arsenal, which the Citizens won 3-0 at Wembley, and De Bruyne claimed his second trophy in English football—but this one was more meaningful as it was the first that he could play in the final for. By comparison, the FA Cup was not as fruitful, as the team was knocked out by Wigan Athletic in the fifth round.

The UEFA Champions League resumed in February 2018 with De Bruyne providing a scrumptious corner kick for Ilkay Gundogan to open the scoring in Switzerland against FC Basel. This led to a 4-0 win on the night and Man City easily progressed to the next round. The next round placed them against a familiar foe in the form of Liverpool. In an out-of-character performance from both De Bruyne and the entire team, City were dumped out of the Champions League as they lost 5-1 on aggregate to their fierce Northwest rivals.

Manchester City and Kevin De Bruyne were officially named Premier League champions for the 2017-18 season when West Bromwich Albion stunned Manchester United at Old Trafford, meaning that nobody could catch their point tally.[lxxx] With this happening in mid-April, and with no other competitions left to compete in, the league title was now secured and Pep Guardiola had the opportunity to rest his players.

But while the league title was already won, De Bruyne and the Manchester City players continued to fight and earn their place in Premier League history. This team from the 2017-18 season was affectionately nicknamed the "Centurions," because the team was the first to earn 100 points across the domestic league season.[lxxxi] Of course, De Bruyne was essential to the team achieving the century point tally as he set up Gabriel Jesus in the last minute of the final game of the season, thus allowing Manchester City to win 1-0 and earn the three points needed to reach the century mark.

The team continued to make history as they also set a slew of impressive Premier League records, including most away points (50), most points ahead of the second-placed team (19), most wins (32), most away wins (16), most goals (106), best goal difference (+79), and most consecutive victories (18).

While nearly every starting player on that amazing squad could rightly be called a hero, Kevin De Bruyne had undeniably been pivotal in the campaign, as he played in 37 of the 38 league games, scored 8 goals, and made 16 assists on the way to claiming his first Premier League winners medal of his career. Given the aforementioned accolades and records that the team had broken and the fact that De Bruyne was almost ever-present, it validated just how critical the talented Belgian player was to the team's successes throughout the season.

Furthermore, compared to the last season, Pep Guardiola now had a much better idea of how he wanted to execute De Bruyne's abilities in the future. This signified having the Belgian play almost exclusively in the midfield positions.

In total, De Bruyne made 52 appearances across all the competitions in the 2017-18 season, making 21 assists and scoring 12 for the team. Despite recording two fewer assists in the league than last season with 16, it was still enough for him to secure the most assists in the league for the 2017-18 season.

2018-19: Injury-Marred Campaign

The early season indicators did not make for pleasant reading for the Man City faithful, as Kevin De Bruyne had sustained an injury that stopped him from playing in pre-season. He was photographed using crutches in various media outlets as it became known that he had picked up an injury during a training session.[lxxxii] He was hoping to start the Premier League game against Arsenal but was then ruled out again for several more weeks.[lxxxiii]

De Bruyne was finally deemed fit enough to come off the bench against Burnley, his first return to the pitch following his pre-season injury.[lxxxiv] His next appearance was in a competitive continental match when he put in a 69-minute performance in the UEFA Champions League group stage, where he provided an assist for Aymeric Laporte against Shakhtar Donetsk.[lxxxv]

De Bruyne then came off the bench in the proceeding Premier League game against Tottenham Hotspur and started the fourth round of the League Cup against Fulham. However, he notably limped off in the latter, leading to him missing another six Premier League games and the remaining UEFA Champions League games.[lxxxvi]

Given the importance of the season and the obvious conclusion that Kevin was still on the mend, Pep decided to not thrust the returning player straight back into the Premier League. Instead, De Bruyne would play a bigger role in the League Cup campaign when he scored the goal against Leicester City in the quarter-final tie, which the team won on penalties.

Of course, Kevin would certainly have wanted the beginning of 2019 to be a fresh start for him, having spent the best part of the previous season struggling with an injury. However, that did not quite transpire, as he picked up a fresh muscle injury that led him to miss games against Southampton and Liverpool.[lxxxvii]

His next starting match appearance came in the empathetic 9-0 victory against Burton Albion in the League Cup semi-final. Up 5-0 with nearly an hour played, Pep decided to take the recovering Belgian off the field to safeguard his health. Kevin was not happy to be retired from the game so early, however, as he actively stormed off the pitch and down the tunnel. Clearly, he had wanted to play more of the game.[lxxxviii] Ironically, this game turned out to be his biggest career win to date. Manchester City ended up winning the tie 10-0 on aggregate and advanced to another League Cup final.

This victory led to a date with Chelsea for De Bruyne and company at Wembley to play for the trophy. The game itself, expected to be a thriller, turned out to be nothing of the sort. In fact, it was notable for a lack of shots throughout the match. It eventually went to penalties as it finished 0-0. De Bruyne was substituted off for Leroy Sane in the 86th minute as Guardiola tried to win the game. While Sane's involvement did not have a major impact on the result, City still won the shoot-out and lifted the trophy in victory.

Frankly, Kevin De Bruyne did not look like himself in the latter parts of the Premier League. Thus, Pep had to ensure heavy rotation as he tried to win all competitions and did not want to rush the Belgian back after his woeful injury record for the season. Despite his burning desire to play, it was apparent at times that their prized midfielder had been struggling and still suffering the effects of those injuries. And, as it turned out, further complications with his thigh and hamstring would keep him out of future games.[lxxxix]

De Bruyne came on as a late substitute in the final game of the season against Brighton and Hove Albion in a game that Manchester City needed to win to lift the title. With only 12 minutes left to play, and by the time De Bruyne was on the field, Man City was already up 4-1, and the result stood as the team retained the Premier League title.[xc]

After winning the Premier League title, De Bruyne appeared noticeably rejuvenated in his post-match interview.

"I feel very honored to be here today … When I had the injury against Tottenham, the first thing I said to the physios was. 'Leave me alone; I want to go on holiday; I'm done.' … I switched after a week and wanted to be ready to help the team if necessary … It feels special because we've gone back to back."[xci]

His injuries had kept him out of the first knockout round of the second leg of the UEFA Champions League against FC Schalke 04. However, the resounding 7-0 win with De Bruyne out of the team suggested that this team was now well-stacked. This made up a 10-2 aggregate win as they advanced to the quarter-final phase with relative ease.

Just like the season prior, Manchester City were paired against English opposition in continental competition. This time, they had to contest the quarter-final against Tottenham Hotspur. De Bruyne played just a single minute of the away leg in London as a very late substitute. Son-Heung Min scored the only goal of the game (even with Sergio Aguero missing a penalty earlier in the night) as Tottenham took a 1-0 lead in the second leg in Manchester.

The proceeding leg turned out to be a jarring night for all involved with the Sky Blue Citizens, and especially for De Bruyne. While he pulled off a hat-trick of assists, having set up both Raheem Sterling and Sergio Aguero, the result was still not in the team's favor. The 4-3 score meant that Manchester City would exit the competition on away goals again.[xcii]

There was still a personal milestone for Kevin De Bruyne that year, even if he did not play in too many games throughout the season. This special moment came in the FA Cup competition, the one and only English football trophy that De Bruyne had not won at this juncture in his now-storied career.

De Bruyne started the campaign by captaining the team against Rotherham United in a spectacular 7-0 victory. The next match was another resounding victory for Manchester City as De Bruyne scored and assisted two goals against Burnley in a 5-0 win. KDB missed the next two matches against Newport County and Swansea City. However, Man City still progressed to the semi-finals.

The semi-final match pitted Manchester City against Brighton and Hove Albion. Kevin De Bruyne played 65 minutes of the game and provided a critical assist for Gabriel Jesus, as the game ended 1-0 for the Citizens (who would advance to the final against Watford). Despite the prior match being tightly contested between the teams, the final was anything but.

De Bruyne entered the field at 55 minutes when Manchester City were already up 2-0. The Belgian contributed a goal and an assist (both combined with Gabriel Jesus) as the final ended 6-0 and De Bruyne got his hands on the FA Cup trophy for the first time.

Even though De Bruyne only played 35 minutes of the game, his superb efforts were such that he was still named the man of the match.

De Bruyne summarized the season after collecting his winner's medal. "It has been an unbelievable season to win three titles ... It says enough ... We are happy with what we have done this season and we are happy to be in the conversation, but we should just enjoy the moment because it doesn't happen very often . . It is not about topping it; it is about being consistent and trying to achieve the best

… We are not starting the season saying we want to win three titles or four titles, we want to play the way we play and do our best … It is not all about the end product; it is about the journey and you appreciate it even more … It does (mean a lot) because I wanted to end in a good way. It has been a stop-start season for me, and it has been difficult at times … I wanted to show the people I am still the same player, I just had some bad luck this season. Now everyone knows I am the same and go into the summer in the right way."[xciii]

Ultimately, De Bruyne would have been glad to see the end of the 2018-19 campaign, given that he had suffered multiple injuries and related setbacks throughout the season. He only made 19 appearances in the Premier League and scored just two goals, definitely well below his usual standards. He did pick up three winners medals for the season, however, from the Premier League, the FA Cup, and the League Cup triumphs.

Even in a season where he was repeatedly injured, De Bruyne still made 32 appearances across all the competitions in the season. He showed a desire to contribute and, as such, still accumulated 11 assists and 6 goals, vindicating his spot in the team even if his playtime was drastically reduced.

2019-20: Improved Season Amidst COVID

To prepare for the 2019-20 season, Manchester City went to East Asia, where they played a rich variety of different teams in China, Hong Kong, and Japan. The last game of the pre-season was against the

City Group affiliate team, Yokohama F. Marinos Kevin De Bruyne opened the scoring in this match, one of his very few pre-season goals to date in a game that ended 3-1 to the English team.[xciv]

The competitive season started with a 1-1 draw in the Community Shield against Liverpool. De Bruyne was substituted in the 89th minute for Phil Foden. Manchester City would eventually win the game via a penalty shoot-out. The start of the Premier League 2019-20 season proved to be an imperious run for the Belgian midfielder. It appeared that he was trying to make up for lost time, having endured an awful spate of injuries in the previous season His five assists in the opening four games ensured that the team progressed well.

The Champions League group stage placed Manchester City against Shakhtar Donetsk, Dinamo Zagreb, and Atalanta, a group which Manchester City would be considered favorites to progress from. De Bruyne was quiet on the group stage, as he only played four games. His only direct goal involvement came in the first game, where he connected with Gabriel Jesus as the match ended 3-0 at the expense of the Ukrainian team. Manchester City would qualify from the group with relative ease.

While a small injury did arise during the infancy of the season, a small ankle problem only ruled him out of a few games.[xcv] After missing the match against Wolverhampton Wanderers, De Bruyne started to bolster his goal tally in the Premier League, scoring against Chelsea and Newcastle United in consecutive matches.

41

Uncharacteristically, De Bruyne was rotated from the League Cup competition and did not feature in any of the first three rounds.

De Bruyne signed off 2019 in great style as he scored twice against Arsenal in a 3-0 win at Emirates Stadium. That was then followed by three assists and another goal in the subsequent games. The year 2020 started in good fashion for the Belgian too, as he made two assists in the 6-1 win at Villa Park against Aston Villa. De Bruyne has since stated that he believes this was his best-ever performance for Manchester City.[xcvi]

The attacking midfielder played 80 minutes in the first leg of the League Cup semi-final against Manchester United. He picked up yet another assist there, and Manchester City left Old Trafford as 3-1 winners. De Bruyne won the captain's armband for the home match, and while the visitors might have won 1-0 on the night, City would still progress to the League Cup final via the 3-2 aggregate score.

The League Cup final was contested against Aston Villa at Wembley Stadium. De Bruyne did not start the game but did play the last half hour. At the time of his arrival on the pitch, the score was 2-1 and that would be the way it would finish as he got his hands on yet another trophy.

The Round of 16 paired Manchester City up with Real Madrid. The first game in Madrid was a drab affair with little action. De Bruyne may have just been taking his time to strike when he set up Gabriel

Jesus for an equalizer. Five minutes later, the Belgian scored from a penalty kick to take a winning aggregate back to Manchester.

Come the start of March, De Bruyne suffered a back and shoulder injury which forced him out of the Manchester derby.[xcvii] No matter the severity of his injury, De Bruyne had three months to rest and recover, as the global COVID-19 pandemic ensured that even football had to be paused.[xcviii]

When the Premier League was able to continue its operations, Manchester City took center stage, participating in the first wave of fixtures to be played as part of the operation restart.[xcix] De Bruyne scored from the penalty spot as Manchester City defeated Arsenal 3-0. De Bruyne would keep providing goals for the team, notching up scores against Chelsea and Liverpool, and bagging a brace against Norwich City on the final day of the season.

While Man City tried to apply pressure, it was clear by an early part of the restart that Liverpool would win the 2019-20 season. Manchester City finished in second place. De Bruyne did, however, claim the Premier League Player of the Season Award, which gave him some personal recognition.[c]

The award was bestowed upon De Bruyne for his tremendous season, as he provided 20 assists in the Premier League for his teammates. This incredible tally would match the record for most assists from an individual player in a single season, as only the legendary Thierry Henry also set up 20 goals in the 2002-03 season.[ci]

The UEFA Champions League campaign also needed to be resumed with safety restrictions in place to help slow the spread of the rampaging COVID-19 virus. UEFA allowed the participating domestic competitions to finish and then complete the competition on a World Cup tournament-style basis in one set location to reduce the chance of infection.

As Manchester City had already played the first leg of their tie against Real Madrid, they had to finish the preset rules and deliver another 2-1 win. But the next round provided a real shock to the football world as Olympique Lyon ended any hope of a City victory. The upstart French team won the revised single-game tie 3-1. De Bruyne had scored an equalizer in the 69th minute to take the game to 1-1, however, Moussa Dembele proceeded to score two more, ensuring victory for the French team.

At the conclusion of this unusual season, De Bruyne played 48 games across both domestic and continental club competitions. In these efforts, he was able to score 16 goals and set up a further 23 for his teammates.

2020-21: Captaining the Team, Lifting Trophies

Given the late finish to the 2019-20 season, English football had a very short break of only four weeks before the next season would commence. Despite that, Kevin De Bruyne started the season in amazing style as he scored and assisted against the Wolverhampton Wanderers in the opening game. Due to Fernandinho's advancing years, the captain's armband became increasingly commonplace on De Bruyne as the veteran Brazilian was swapped out. The 2020-21 season would be remembered as one of the most taxing for the players due to the fixture congestion along with the added risks of COVID-19 infection as the pandemic lingered on.

De Bruyne only played two of the UEFA Champions League group stage matches due to the aforementioned fixture congestion. He did provide four assists in those two games against Olympique Marseille and Olympiacos. While these results are not the totality of the team qualifying for the knockout stage, they certainly put Manchester City in the right position to do so. Similarly, De Bruyne was also used in passing during the earlier rounds of the League Cup—however, the team still won its games.

Kevin De Bruyne ended the year with the armband around his bicep and was quite prolific for Manchester City in the Premier League. He was, at times, unplayable during December as he racked up multiple consecutive assists. In a gratifying moment, he even scored against his former employers, Chelsea.

By comparison, January was not as good for De Bruyne as he incurred a hamstring injury that sidelined him for six weeks.[cii] His manager, Pep Guardiola, labeled him as an irreplaceable player. "We're going to miss him a lot … He's almost irreplaceable with the quality he has. He was nominated the best player in the Premier League last season so we know how good he is."[ciii]

The Belgian was back in time for the second leg of their UEFA Champions League last 16 tie against Borussia Monchengladbach. With a 2-0 advantage on aggregate, De Bruyne returned to the starting eleven with a goal and helped the team secure another 2-0 win. Borussia Dortmund fought harder against Man City in the quarter-final but also came up short as De Bruyne scored again in a tie that ended 4-2.

Back in the Premier League, Guardiola essentially wrapped De Bruyne in cotton wool. He had already won the English title many times, and while he wanted to retain the title, he believed that resting De Bruyne in this competition as much as possible would give him a better chance of winning the Champions League trophy. De Bruyne notably scored two goals in the 5-2 win against Southampton, and then again in the 5-0 win on the final day of the season against Everton. City retained the title with consistent performances and Manchester United, the second-place team, slipped in the title race and lost to Leicester, meaning that City would lead the league with three games left to play.[civ]

The semi-final of the UEFA Champions League beckoned, and Man City had to face a resilient Paris Saint-Germain team, which was stacked with terrific talent. De Bruyne proved to be the catalyst in this game as he scored the equalizer in Paris, and that led to the team winning the away leg. They followed it up with a 2-0 home win, ensuring a 4-1 aggregate to secure the club's first-ever Champions League final appearance.

The final against Chelsea was held at Estadio do Dragao in Porto, which would host a smaller number of fans (which was necessary because the ongoing COVID-19 restrictions limited attendance).

De Bruyne was substituted off after 60 minutes as he picked up a collision injury that resulted in a trip to the hospital. The team was down 1-0 at that point and that was how it stayed, thus, their English opposition won the trophy at City's expense.

In the wake of the match, De Bruyne revealed that he did not recall much of the game. "I don't remember after the incident so there's not a lot of memories ... In these games you can lose; the opposition is very good; that night we lost and move on ... I remember some chances in the first half, but after the collision, I don't remember a lot, about how I got into the hospital. I remember going back in the morning to the hotel at 10 a.m. still with my kit on ... In sport, it happens. It's not the best thing to happen but you go on with it."[cv] He later added that this game would not define his career.[cvi]

At the end of the season, Sergio Aguero left Manchester City after a 10-year association with the club. The Argentinian player was heralded as a hero for his exceptional performances and his longstanding dedication to the team. During his exit, he also paid homage to KDB. "For me, Kevin De Bruyne is one of the best midfielders in the world ... It was always so special to play with Kevin De Bruyne because he was so good at moving the ball exactly where he wanted it. He only needs one look to know where you are or where you are going to move and he'll get the ball to you immediately; his speed and accuracy with passing is like nobody else."[cvii]

This season saw De Bruyne take the unusual role of center-forward, a position he had rarely played since his early days with Werder Bremen. KDB ended up playing in a much more advanced position in nine distinct games toward the tail end of the season. This run of games saw him score four goals as he tailored his game to be more striking. He made no assists in these games in which he played as a CF. When asked about playing in this role, De Bruyne stated that it was a different situation but he was willing to help his team in any capacity.

"It was a bit bizarre in the beginning, I've done it a few times in my career; obviously, we have a lot of forwards out and the coach asked me to do this job, so I tried my best to do it as good as possible."[cviii]

In totality, De Bruyne played 40 games throughout the entire season, scoring 10 goals and assisting 18 more.

2021-22: De Bruyne Masterclass

The 2021-22 season could not have started any worse for Kevin De Bruyne. The European Championship campaign saw him suffer a niggling ankle injury, and he subsequently missed the Community Shield fixture against Leicester City, a game that Manchester City lost without him.

He was then tested in the first match of the Premier League season but only lasted 11 minutes before being substituted.[cix] To make matters even worse, Tottenham went on to win that game 1-0. After missing about a month of action, he was finally back and ready to dissect opposition defenses. For most of the early season, Pep played De Bruyne in a more central role as opposed to the attacking midfield role he was famous for.

This season, De Bruyne did not see a lot of the captain's armband, as Ilkay Gundogan and Ruben Dias were selected over the Belgian for leadership duties. De Bruyne returned from his ankle injury to score in consecutive matches against Liverpool and Burnley. Now with a competent slew of quality teammates around him, the truth was that De Bruyne did not need to play every top-tier game. Instead, he was used as a bit-part player in the group stage of the UEFA Champions League; the team easily qualified from the group, which also contained RB Leipzig, Paris Saint-Germain, and Club Brugge.

De Bruyne was also afforded a good chunk of time off to recover from a COVID-19 infection.[cx] His first start after his absence came in the 7-0 mauling of Leeds United where he played 90 minutes and scored two goals in the process. However, in a post-match interview, he revealed that, even after that performance, he was still suffering. "After COVID, I came back and trained as hard as I could. With the schedule, it is not that easy but I'm doing all right. I played in two games and came on as a sub in two, so I'm doing what I need to do …

I still feel sometimes that my body is adapting because I do two or three sprints and feel it, having had COVID."[cxi]

De Bruyne may not have been feeling his best but he was still paramount to Manchester City going on an eight-game winning streak throughout the winter months. He would also provide critical passes in the build-up play in the proceeding UEFA Champions League games; the team had to deal with two Iberian teams, firstly Sporting Lisbon and then Atletico Madrid. De Bruyne provided a direct goal contribution against each as they motored into the semi-final against Real Madrid.

The first game of the UEFA Champions League has to go down in the annals as one of the best soccer games ever played.[cxii] Manchester City won the game 4-3 with De Bruyne putting in a real shift, as he scored after two minutes of play and provided an assist for Gabriel Jesus. The second match wasn't as fruitful, however. De Bruyne did not seem to be himself at Bernabeu and was taken off after 72 minutes. Real Madrid forced the tie to extra time and ended up progressing. The agony of that UEFA Champions League loss would continue for De Bruyne and Manchester City.

Unfortunately, neither domestic cup saw any success. De Bruyne sat on the bench in the FA Cup semi-final as Liverpool defeated City. And then, uncharacteristically, the League Cup saw the team exit at an early stage via penalties to West Ham United. De Bruyne played throughout the match but was taken off toward the end to facilitate an appearance from Jack Grealish.

Luckily, Manchester City had the Premier League competition to fall back on. De Bruyne finished the league in white-hot form, scoring for fun as the team closed in on another piece of silverware. This included a famous 4-1 win over Manchester United in which the Belgian scored twice. However, that paled in comparison to the match against the Wolverhampton Wanderers in which he scored four!

The Belgian backed himself in the post-match interview. "The third goal was my favorite. I think that strike is the cleanest. I hit it hard in the corner. Out of the three, that was the purest ... When you score four goals, it's always something special. It should have been five, to be honest!"[cxiii] This individual performance from De Bruyne has since been praised as one of the best in the annals of the entire Premier League.[cxiv]

The Premier League title would be decided on the final day of the season, with Liverpool sitting only one point below Manchester City. Aston Villa remarkably raced into a 2-0 lead at the Etihad, but that would not be the end of the story.[cxv] Instead, with 14 minutes left to play, Manchester City forced their way back into the game. This culminated in De Bruyne securing his eighth assist of the season when his ball found Ilkay Gundogan for a thrilling, critical combination play that saw Manchester City win 3-2 and retain the Premier League title.[cxvi]

Manchester City celebrated the title win with an obligatory open-top bus parade around multiple areas of the city. De Bruyne stated that he had a drink or two in celebration of the title win. "I'm a little bit drunk! It's amazing to do this for the fourth time and amazing to see so many people here to celebrate with us. Thank you to the fans, the last game and atmosphere was amazing. Enjoy the summer and let's go again."[cxvii]

The 2021-22 season has become known as one of the most prolific campaigns for Kevin De Bruyne. Across all 45 appearances he made, the Belgian scored 19 goals and assisted another 14, further cementing his legacy at the club. Pep Guardiola applauded his star midfielder and commented on his successes in the campaign. "He is not just a player to make assists—now he scores a lot of goals. I've said to him many times, 'I know you enjoy making a lot of assists for you and your team-mates, but you have to score goals to reach another stage … Now he is doing that, a lot of goals and chances."[cxviii]

2022-23: Treble-Winning Season

At the start of the 2022-23 season, there was a great deal of conjecture as to who would still be at Manchester City. Kevin De Bruyne had played a lot of games with teammates Raheem Sterling and Gabriel Jesus. He had made 60 joint goal contributions with these players. Therefore, it was surprising when Manchester City sold both players in the summer of 2022 to Chelsea and Arsenal, respectively.

This transfer activity was to facilitate the emergence of a new signing, Erling Haaland.[cxix] Out of the two players who were departing, De Bruyne was more concerned that the Brazilian would be leaving, having tried to get him to stay in the summer.

"Since he [Jesus] came here, I've had a good relationship with him," De Bruyne said. "I think we've found each other lots of times. He plays with so much energy, he's always there, and he helps the team out. I have never had any doubts about his quality and he's still so young. I hope he can play many times with me because I think he makes this team better."[cxx]

This sentiment was perhaps at odds with how Kevin felt about Raheem Sterling, however, as De Bruyne had initially thought he was not the nicest of people.[cxxi] However, De Bruyne later stated that his initial thoughts about the Englishman had been wrong, stating, "Raheem is one of the nicest, most humble guys I've met in football … Truthfully, I don't have many close friends—inside or outside of football. It takes me a long time to open up to people. But over time, I got closer to Raheem, because our sons were born around the same time, so they would always play together."[cxxii] Sterling would end up being De Bruyne's most consistent teammate, as the two played 243 times together.

The first match of the 2022-23 season pitted Manchester City against Liverpool in the Community Shield. De Bruyne played 73 minutes in a game that did not go to plan for the Citizens, as they lost 3-1.

Despite that initial setback, the Belgian and the rest of the team soon bounced back, with De Bruyne hitting marvelous form straight out of the gate. He made four direct goal contributions in the first three games. He then kept up the same form as he assisted in the first two UEFA Champions League group stage victories against Sevilla FC and Borussia Dortmund. Manchester City went undefeated throughout the league with four wins and two losses as the team topped the Group G standings.

De Bruyne appeared in imperious fashion through most of the season. One of his most prolific sequences came in the early autumnal months when his efforts allowed the team to record empathetic victories against the Wolverhampton Wanderers, Manchester United, and Southampton in the Premier League.

Come the end of the calendar year, the Premier League was celebrating its 30th year since its inception. As such, the team tried to commemorate and recognize some of the greatest players to play in the top flight of English football since 1992. Kevin De Bruyne was voted the best midfielder in Premier League history, eclipsing the likes of Steven Gerrard, Paul Scholes, and Frank Lampard.[cxxiii]

Pep Guardiola rotated his team heavily for the League Cup match against Southampton, the team that was sitting at the bottom of the Premier League at this point in early January. Manchester City were 2-0 down after 28 minutes of play, and Pep made more changes to his team at the half-time break. That was when De Bruyne was introduced to the match, but not even his supreme abilities were able to break a resolute, win-hungry Southampton team on the night.

The other domestic cup competition, the FA Cup, proved to be a lot more productive for the team. City won every match, however, De Bruyne only recorded his first major contribution in the fifth round of the tournament when he scored against Bristol City. Then he made two assists against Burnley in the subsequent round. The Belgian midfielder was not required for the semi-final tie against Sheffield United, as he sat on the bench for the entirety of the contest.

De Bruyne did, however, play a major part in the final, assisting both goals for Ilkay Gundogan to defeat Manchester United 2-1 at Wembley Stadium. After the match and lifting the FA Cup, De Bruyne commented on the successes. "It's been an incredible season and hopefully we can make it even better."[cxxiv] His comment was a clear indication that the team wanted to win yet more silverware.

Manchester City continued to be in electric form throughout the Premier League season, winning multiple matches with large scorelines. Kevin De Bruyne became simply untouchable in April 2023 when he recorded three goals and five assists in a four-game series in which they defeated their closest title rival, Arsenal, 4-1. They were then announced as Premier League champions, as Arsenal subsequently lost a game to Nottingham Forest, thereby gifting City the title with three games to spare.[cxxv]

When the UEFA Champions League resumed with the knockout stages, Manchester City first had an away game against RB Leipzig. However, De Bruyne would not make the flight to Germany when an undisclosed illness ruled him out of the game.[cxxvi] He did, however, have a large part in the home leg as Manchester City won 7-0, ensuring an 8-1 aggregate win and passage to the next round. De Bruyne then helped Pep Guardiola overcome his old team, Bayern Munich, as he provided an assist in the 4-1 aggregate win and helped Manchester City book their place in the semi-final.

In a cagey first-leg at the Santiago Bernabéu, Kevin De Bruyne scored one of the most important goals of his career. His right-footed shot ensured that Manchester City took a 1-1 draw into the second leg back in England. He then became the goal assistor in that match when he combined with both Bernardo Silva and Manuel Akanji. The contest ended 4-0 for City and they advanced to the final of the UEFA Champions League.

De Bruyne and company next awaited Inter Milan at the Atatürk Olympic Stadium in Istanbul, Turkey. A lot of the pre-match speculation followed De Bruyne's untimely injury during the 2021 final and some people wondered if Manchester City would *ever* win this specific trophy. Only adding to that speculation, 36 minutes into the match, a freak occurrence took place as De Bruyne would yet again have to be substituted off in the biggest match in club football![cxxvii] Unlike the prior final, however, Manchester City went on to win the match, as a slender 1-0 result defeated the opposition.

In the aftermath of winning the trophy, De Bruyne commented, "Hearing the words *Champions League winner* sounds good. I don't know, my head feels a little bit empty for the moment. It's just amazing. It's incredible … It's probably both relief and joy because there's always the pressure when you have never done it to do it and now we have … But we've not lost one game in the Champions League this season so I think we deserve it."[cxxviii]

De Bruyne added that it was unfortunate that he could not play the full match and was not able to be on the pitch when the winning goal was scored. "I've been struggling with the injury since Bayern Munich away … It was all small ruptures but here I snapped it all the way. I've been told for two months there's a possibility I was at risk but, you know, you take it … I was there for my team and did what I needed to do. I missed some games but the games like Arsenal, Bayern, and Madrid … I managed to do it. I had some personal things that happened with my family on top of that and I managed that. It's a shame it went the way it did for me but we go away winning the Champions League so there's nothing bad about it."[cxxix]

De Bruyne also added that the team had installed a winning mentality within the ranks. "We like to win, and we're never bored of it. We've won a lot in the past but we want to win again and again."[cxxx]

While Kevin De Bruyne is known to be an introvert and not partial to drinking alcohol, amid the historic UEFA Champions League win, he could be seen dancing in the post-match celebrations and even had a beer in hand at some points.[cxxxi]

Erling Haaland, the team's newest acquisition, was praised as one of the heroes of the treble-winning season, as he had scored multiple goals throughout the campaign. However, the talismanic Norwegian attributed lots of praise to Kevin De Bruyne for his successes. "I know that when Kevin De Bruyne has the ball, I have to be on the opposite side in the right place and at the right time for him to play the ball into my course with a sharp cross."[cxxxii]

The sharp crosses and accurate passes had kept coming all season long. Kevin De Bruyne made a grand total of 31 assists in the 49 games he played throughout the 2022-23 season. In addition to those, he also scored a further 10 goals as he helped the team achieve this landmark season.

Chapter 2: International Career

Early Days with Belgium

Kevin De Bruyne is an icon of the Belgian national soccer team. However, he did have to decide to play for the country. He was also eligible to play for the African nation of Burundi, as his mother grew up there before moving to Belgium.[cxxxiii]

Kevin seldom played in international youth competitions because he was already so skilled as a teenager that he was quickly selected for the senior team. In November 2008, De Bruyne made his debut for the Belgian U18 setup. However, six months later and still just 17 years old, he was playing with the U19 team as well. He made his senior debut in an international friendly against Finland in August 2010, a 1-0 loss, as he was selected by Georges Leekens. Interestingly, that cap came before his U21 selection.

Despite his initial call-up in 2010, it took a further two years for him to be regularly involved with the Belgian national team. He scored his first international goal and recorded an assist in a 3-0 victory over Serbia. He kept up this form and became integra_ to the 2014 World Cup qualification campaign. De Bruyne's four goals in this qualification phase ensured that Belgium topped their group and would book their ticket to the tournament in Brazil.

The 2014 World Cup in Brazil

The international friendlies in the lead-up to the 2014 World Cup proved to be a purple patch for De Bruyne, as he provided assists for the national team in four consecutive matches against Japan, the Ivory Coast, Luxembourg, and Switzerland. The World Cup itself pitted De Bruyne and company against Algeria, Russia, and South Korea—a group from which they would be expected to qualify.

Despite going 1-0 in their opening game against Algeria, De Bruyne provided an expert quality cross for the towering Marouane Fellaini to head the goal home for 1-1. Belgium would then go on to win the match 2-1. De Bruyne was rested for the third match when the second result (a win 1-0 over Russia) meant that the team had already qualified for the knockout stage.

The Round of 16 match against the U.S. proved to be one of De Bruyne's most exceptional performances in his national colors. The game went to extra time as it was deadlocked at 0-0 after 90 minutes, yet this served as a wake-up call for De Bruyne. Five minutes into the additional period, he hit a wicked ball with great venom past multiple American defenders and the hapless Tim Howard right into the opposition's net. He then laced through an exceptional pass for Romelu Lukaku, who put Belgium up 2-0 and assured that they went on to win 2-1.

Argentina was the next opponent for Belgium in the quarter-final, yet the game was a ho-hum affair; Gonzalo Higuain scored the only goal in the eighth minute and thus, Kevin De Bruyne's first major international tournament ended.

2016 European Championships

Now considered a major part of the national team, De Bruyne was selected to the starting eleven for every competitive game as Marc Wilmots continued his tenure as the national team coach. De Bruyne was pivotal in the subsequent 2016 UEFA European Championship qualification group, notching up five goals in their group. He notably scored two against Andorra in a game that Belgium won 6-0. Such results and performances ensured that Belgium topped their qualification group.

De Bruyne played every minute of the tournament in France. The team came unstuck in the opening game against Italy with a 2-0 loss, [cxxxiv]meaning that De Bruyne was needed in all three games. Kevin provided a critical assist in the match against the Republic of Ireland and the team managed to qualify. De Bruyne would follow that clutch performance up in the Round of 16, where he combined with both Toby Alderweireld and Eden Hazard to earn two assists in a 4-0 victory. The next match proved to be one of the biggest upsets in UEFA national football history, however, as Wales won 3-1 in Lille, France.[cxxxv]

In the aftermath of the shocking defeat, Kevin De Bruyne was vocal in his criticism of the manager, Marc Wilmots. "Why did we drop off? Why did we give them the chance to take charge? ... In the end, it's the coach who decides how we play and who takes the decisions."[cxxxvi]

Wilmots tried to explain why key players like De Bruyne did not perform as expected and speculated that, in the case of Kevin, his transfer to Manchester City may have affected his abilities. "He was transferred for a lot of money and there are a lot of things going on in his life."[cxxxvii]

But Wilmots's defensive counterpoints held little sway, and the loss to Wales proved to be the final straw. Wilmot would soon be relieved of his duties by the Belgian FA, as they decided it was time to take a new direction in their leadership. He was thus replaced with the former Everton and Wigan Athletic manager, Roberto Martinez.[cxxxviii]

Heroic Performances at the 2018 World Cup

Unsurprisingly, and having seen De Bruyne's quality in the Premier League, the new Spanish manager continued to select Kevin for the national team. However, multiple injuries to De Bruyne's hamstring and groin that he suffered during this time ultimately stopped him from being involved in the infancy of Martinez's reign.

In the build-up to the 2018 World Cup, Belgium went on a 12-game unbeaten streak across the qualification phase and several international friendlies. Kevin de Bruyne played the majority of minutes available in those games, notably scoring and assisting two against Saudia Arabia. During this phase, Martinez tinkered with the starting eleven and put De Bruyne in a more defensive midfield position role, something that was foreign to De Bruyne at club level.[cxxxix] At the time, De Bruyne was critical of the new coach and his methods, believing that his tactics were too defensive.[cxl] KDB did, however, note that he thought the team had developed with the prior experiences at international tournaments, and that would help them to stay calm and advance further in the 2018 World Cup.[cxli]

Belgium subsequently brought the same form and success into the tournament in Russia, defeating Panama 3-0 and Tunisia 5-2. As the tournament progressed, there was an unusual happenstance in Group G where the runner-up of the table would get an "easier" route to the final, meaning that they would be pitted against opponents who were classically weaker in world football.[cxlii] Therefore, the last match between Belgium and England took an unusual turn—in short, neither team wanted to win! Roberto Martinez even stated that "defeating England is not a priority."[cxliii] As such, De Bruyne played no part in that match, although a rotated Belgium team still emerged as 1-0 winners.

The Round of 16 games put De Bruyne and Belgium against Japan. KDB and many of the superstars of the team put in a disappointing performance throughout that match as Japan raced to a 2-0 lead.[cxliv] But the tactical prowess of Roberto Martinez from the dugout paid off, as Belgium came back to win 3-2 within the final seconds of stoppage time.

De Bruyne then made up for his lackluster performance in the next match when he scored the crucial goal in the quarter-final against Brazil in a 2-1 victory. De Bruyne was subsequently named the Man of the Match against the South American juggernauts for his efforts.

In a post-match interview, he stated just how hard it was to craft out this result. "It is not easy to play against Brazil, they are such a wonderful team ... But the power we have as a team has shown today, especially in the first half. I think we played magnificently ... The second half was very difficult, and the last 15 minutes were a character test, but I think we showed the world what we are capable of."[cxlv]

The semi-final was a drawn-out contest against France where even Kevin De Bruyne struggled to get the ball moving up the pitch.

France would win the game 1-0. Belgium, while slightly dejected at the loss to the French, would play England again in the third-place playoff match and claim the bronze medal. In the post-tournament conjecture, De Bruyne was named among FIFA's dream team of the 2018 tournament.[cxlvi]

Given De Bruyne's injuries after the summer of 2018, his next appearance for the national team was 11 months after the last game in the World Cup. In June 2019, he re-emerged for the squad for the games against Kazakhstan and Scotland. In the latter game, he proved to be the kingpin at King Baudouin Stadium as all the creative play went through him and Belgium earned an impressive 3-0 victory. Martinez then entrusted De Bruyne with the captain's armband for the next international break for the matches against San Marino and Scotland.

The Scottish would come to despise De Bruyne as he again controlled the game with masterful skill, essentially silencing Hampden Park with three first-half assists and even a goal at the end, ending the bout with a 4-0 win in Glasgow, a trouncing courtesy of the KDB show! This form continued but haphazardly, as Kevin's injuries remained to niggle at him, eventually excluding him from several squad call-ups.

Euro 2020 Campaign

Kevin De Bruyne was not named in the starting eleven of Belgium's first match of the 2020 European Championship (held in 2021 due to the COVID-19 pandemic) as he was reportedly still suffering from a facial fracture following a frightening collision with Chelsea's Rudiger in the Champions League final.[cxlvii] He watched from the sidelines as his team defeated Russia 3-0. Then, in the second match, he was still on the bench, even though he had significantly healed. But, with Denmark winning 1-0 at halftime, a desperate Roberto Martinez turned to De Bruyne, as he needed to harness his abilities to turn the game around. And De Bruyne did not disappoint. Within less than 10 minutes of being on the pitch he had provided an assist for Thorgan Hazard to level the game, and then later scored himself to wrap up a 2-1 victory.

To keep up his fitness, KDB played the final group stage game against Finland, which Belgium won 2-0. Despite starting the Round of 16 match, he was forced off the field after sustaining yet another injury.[cxlviii] There was some relief, however, given that Belgium still won the match. De Bruyne was then able to start and play for the entire quarter-final match against Italy but failed to impact the game, as Italy won 2-1 and advanced.

De Bruyne has since stated that he wished he had not rushed to play in the tournament, as he was probably not fit or recovered enough to participate in the competition. He noted that he had to rely on painkillers to get through games, and this led to him having further injury issues. "I came in with an injury to my eye socket [from the Champions League final] and, after three matches, I left with an even more serious ankle injury."[cxlix]

A Disappointing Qatari Campaign

Ahead of the 2022 World Cup, Kevin De Bruyne professed that certain elements of playing with the national team had become relatively tedious to him. This was said ahead of a UEFA Nations League match against Wales, a team which De Bruyne stated he has played at least 12 times before and that he is bored of playing against.[cl]

The 2022 World Cup in Qatar was potentially the lowest level ebb of contemporary Belgian football as the team limped out of the tournament at the group stage with just a solitary win. Before the tournament, De Bruyne also stated that the team, as a collective, was "too old" and had "no chance of winning the World Cup."[cli] He also added that he thought the national team had gone backward since the team finished third in the 2018 tournament. "I think our chance was 2018. We have a good team, but it is aging … We lost some key players. We have some good new players coming, but they are not at the level other players were in 2018. I see us more as outsiders".[clii]

As it turned out, De Bruyne's assertions were quite prophetic. The first match of the World Cup for Belgium was against Canada, a game in which the only goal scored was by Michy Batshuayi in a 1-0 victory for the Belgians. De Bruyne was actually named the Budweiser Man of the Match at the conclusion, but KDB was rather confused at receiving the award and was critical of himself and the team, commenting, "I don't think I played a great game … I don't know why I got the trophy. Maybe it's because of the name. This was not good enough … We made it difficult for ourselves and stress crept into the team. There was more space than was seen and we used the long ball too often … It has to be better, myself included."[cliii]

De Bruyne failed to contribute a single goal or assist in the next two games, which Belgium failed to win. Subsequently, the team would be knocked out at the group stage with Croatia and Morocco advancing instead.

Kevin De Bruyne was heavily criticized by Belgian media and supporters for his pre-competition comments, lackluster performances, and sullen behavior at the tournament.[cliv] Roberto Martinez would then leave the post as his contract expired.[clv]

The Belgian FA then announced that Italian manager Domenico Tedesco would be the man to take over the head coaching duties of the national team. Kevin De Bruyne had had his issues with Roberto Martinez and, frankly, was not totally enamored with the national approach in the past. However, De Bruyne has since said that Tedesco has "brought back the fun" to competing with the Belgium team.[clvi]

Belgium National Team Legacy

De Bruyne is undoubtedly one of Belgium's most successful footballers to have represented the nation and has even been one of the standout performers during the nation's "golden generation." As of October 2023, De Bruyne has amassed 99 international cups for the country and scored 26 goals in the process. While his tenure with the national team has not coincided with silverware or trophies, he has been a critical part of the journey, despite having been outspokenly critical of the manager and the systems employed by them in the past. As of late 2023, De Bruyne is still regularly selected for the national team and remains one of the most popular Belgian soccer players in history.

Chapter 3: Personal Life

Kevin De Bruyne has openly described himself as an introvert and does not like to discuss his private life away from football in great detail. He admits that, earlier in life, this attribute stopped him from forging closer relationships with people both in and out of football. "If I would meet you four years ago I'd say, 'Hello, how are you?' Then I'd go away … I learned how to manage myself growing up and being with people. It's just maturity. Being an introvert is not always easy."[clvii]

De Bruyne can also be described as a *polyglot* as he speaks numerous languages, including Dutch and French from his native Belgium. In addition, while playing in Germany and England, he was able to learn the local languages and speak them with good proficiency.

Despite the fact that most professional athletes have to stick to a strict diet to ensure peak physical performance, Kevin has many food preferences, including some special treats. De Bruyne once told Manchester City media that he preferred Belgian fries to Belgian chocolate and whenever he visits, he tries to eat some.

But he still takes his nutrition very seriously. At one point, he even worked with Jonny Marsh, a famed footballer nutritionist and chef, to develop a "secret pasta sauce" for a bespoke "Kevin Carbonara" dish which De Bruyne regularly consumes during the season.[clviii] When at home, Kevin is also an accomplished cook. He has said he likes to cook a vegan version of spinach and ricotta cannelloni, and that is one of his go-to recipes.[clix]

De Bruyne is known to not enjoy alcohol overly much but will dabble in the occasional social drink when the opportunity arises. This includes trophy celebrations, holidays, or when he is dining with his wife. His friends have reported that he has a relatively low tolerance towards alcohol as well, and dreads doing shots.[clx] He has said that his preferred drink is a glass of rose wine, but if it is not available and it's not a party, he will do fine with sparkling water.[clxi]

Amongst his friends, De Bruyne is known as the "tumble dryer," as he typically employs a dry sense of humor, especially amongst his social circles on instant messaging services.[clxii] He may enjoy the same kind of humor as his wife, Michele Lacroix. Michele also enjoys moderate fame of her own as an internet personality and, of course, for being married to one of the world's best soccer players. She has regularly been cited as having no real interest in the game, however, she does support her husband when he plays.

The two married in 2017, three years after meeting one another, and have since had three children together. Kevin's eldest, Mason, is now an avid Manchester City fan and has even got a haircut resembling De Bruyne's teammate, Erling Haaland.[clxiii] He has stated that his children love animals and that he regularly takes them to the local zoo.[clxiv]

As well as going to the zoo, De Bruyne clearly has a love for animals. He describes himself as a cat person and has a pet cat named Coco. He regularly posts pictures of Coco on his social media channels.

While contemporary professional athletes are often quick to buy expensive clothes and spend their time partying, De Bruyne enjoys an altogether more wholesome pastime that quite literally takes the cake—since living in England, Kevin started to watch the Great British Bake Off.[clxv] Apparently never missing an episode, he has since started making cakes himself in his free time![clxvi]

De Bruyne does, however, enjoy some classic footballer hobbies. He is known to collect premium and luxury cars. His collection is said to include a Ferrari 448, multiple Mercedes-Benz cars, and a Range Rover.[clxvii] In connection with his love for cars, De Bruyne is also a fan of motorsports, F1 especially. De Bruyne went to the 2022 Belgian Grand Prix and met Christian Horner, who is reportedly a fan of the footballer, despite supporting Coventry City. Horner famously said that De Bruyne could drive the prestigious Red Bull F1 car if he transferred to Coventry![clxviii]

De Bruyne has also devoted considerable time and resources to charitable causes, especially those benefiting disabled people and those with specialized needs. He has worked closely with the Special Olympics committee to raise awareness.[clxix] This even entailed him creating a unique fashion brand called KDB in conjunction with Cult

Eleven, with a significant portion of the profits going to the Special Olympics.

As well as his charitable endeavors, Kevin De Bruyne has also taken an active interest in the world of business. His primary reason for doing so is to ensure financial stability for himself and his family after his football career ends. "If you're lucky you play until 35, 36, and then the money just basically stops ... I've seen a lot of players or heard a lot of stories where people after five years go broke even with the money that we make. I also see how quickly the money can go."

Kevin added that he does not want to be like the status quo of athletes who do not appreciate their financial good fortune and have the potential to end up in monetary woe. "I think probably 99% of football players or athletes, they start so young they don't understand how the money works, how it flows, how quickly it goes and when it's gone, it's gone ... You only start to learn it at 27, or 28 but (by then) I'd been making money for 10 years. I bought a house in Manchester and an apartment in Belgium. But except for that, I didn't do too much ... When you start playing football, you don't think about what's going to happen later. My business is playing football and that's still the main business. But now I've got a family, I've got people to take care of, I've got multiple houses. So I see bills coming in and out ... And you think, 'What's going to happen when I'm done and I don't make the money anymore but the bills keep going?' You need to find a way to make money in another way ... I just had a 'click' where I said 'I think I need to start doing something.'"[clxx]

As such De Bruyne has invested in numerous ventures and companies including health products and a Belgian artificial glass firm.

De Bruyne is also an avid video game player in his free time, as he plays a lot of Fortnite and surprisingly, a lot of NBA video games as well. In 2020, he paired up with Tottenham Hotspur's Dele Alli in a charity game of Fortnite to raise funds for the COVID-19 relief effort.[clxxi]

Chapter 4: Future and Legacy

Throughout his illustrious soccer career, Kevin De Bruyne has collected multiple trophies, honors, and individual accolades. This includes winning the league, cup, and Super Cup in his native Belgium with Genk. After which, he went on to win the cup and Super Cup with Wolfsburg. But it was his move to Manchester City that was the true turning point in his career. At Man City, De Bruyne became fully recognized for his greatness on the pitch and became the soccer star he was destined to be. As a Citizen, Kevin improved his trophy count tenfold. As of the 2022-23 season, the superbly talented and prolific Belgian has lifted two FA Cups, five League Cups, five Premier League titles and of course, the UEFA Champions League win in the 2022-23 season.

The numerous team titles and his countless exceptional performances have also singled him out for individual praise, as De Bruyne has been named the PFA Players' Player of the Year twice, Manchester City Player of the Year as many times, and the Transfermarkt Player of the Season two times. Furthermore, he took third place in the 2022 Ballon d'Or.

Throughout his career, Kevin De Bruyne has enjoyed scoring and assisting goals. However, there are some teams against which he has been exceptionally prolific. He made 11 assists against Southampton and a further 10 against Watford. Unfortunately for De Bruyne, as of the 2023-24 season, both of these teams now reside outside the

Premier League, meaning that he can no longer bank on assists against them. In terms of goals, he's enjoyed tallying up the most against Arsenal, as he has scored eight times against the North London club. Arsenal is also the team he has played the most against, having faced off against them 20 times across his career.

Despite having played Arsenal the most as a club, the individual player whom he has contested the most was better known for his long stint with Liverpool—Roberto Firmino. De Bruyne battled Firmino on 23 separate occasions, often getting the best of the famed striker. The pair first played one another when the Brazilian was on the books at TSG Hoffenheim and De Bruyne was with both Werder Bremen and Wolfsburg. But the two formidable foes are commonly known for their personification of the title race rivalry between Manchester City and Liverpool. The pair also played one another in the quarter-final of the 2018 World Cup when Belgium defeated Brazil 2-1.

De Bruyne's biggest wins in his career have been barn-busting results. The highest was a 9-0 win with Belgium against Gibraltar in 2017, which is only slightly better than his 8-0 victory with Manchester City against Watford.

At this point in his career, Kevin De Bruyne has already paid his dues to Manchester City. He has played a significant role in taking the club from the best in England to UEFA Champions League winners, with consistent personal performances along the way, even when the rest of the team did not perform at the same level.

As we look to the future, it is true that the Belgian started the 2023-24 season with multiple injury issues and there was even some speculation that he might be transferred. However, after four months of rehab following surgery for a torn hamstring, De Bruyne is back on the pitch with Man City and seems poised to be as productive as ever.[clxxii]

De Bruyne is under contract with Manchester City until June 2025 but has been inconsistent with his approach to committing his long-term future to the Citizens. During the saga surrounding the club's UEFA competition ban, he even seemed to indicate he would welcome a move to play at the top level.[clxxiii] However, in the summer of 2023, amid many top players moving to the Saudi Arabian league for lucrative contracts (as Firmino did), De Bruyne insisted that he was not interested in leaving Manchester City.[clxxiv] Should his contract run down or circumstances change, one club that has maintained an interest in signing De Bruyne is Atletico Madrid, who attempted to sign him previously.[clxxv]

Given his commitment to Manchester City and unwavering performance rate, other club icons have stated that Kevin De Bruyne will be one of the first names considered when the club ownership decides to commission new statues to be placed outside the Etihad Stadium, along with Pep Guardiola.[clxxvi]

Many pundits before the 2022-23 UEFA Champions League final stressed that De Bruyne needed a "legacy-defining" moment to forge his career as one of the greatest of all time.[clxxvii] While critics would point out that, while Manchester City won the match, the Belgian was not on the field when the team went ahead. When De Bruyne was quizzed on the importance of that particular match, he downplayed the significance of the marquee fixture. "It depends who you ask … Will it help, yes. But one 90 minutes doesn't define a career. I am on around 700 games. One 90 minutes out of 700 doesn't define my career. But obviously, it helps."[clxxviii]

With or without the medals, there is no disputing that De Bruyne has had a tremendous impact on Manchester City, English football, and the wider sport in general. In 2017, Roberto Martinez, KDB's national team manager, stated that De Bruyne could be as prolific and as successful as elite players like Lionel Messi and Cristiano Ronaldo.[clxxix]

While comparisons to players typically played in different positions can be hard to assess, De Bruyne has now been rated above many of the legendary midfielders to have ever participated in the Premier League. He was also voted the best Premier League midfielder of all time, as he eclipsed players like Steven Gerrard, Frank Lampard, and even Paul Scholes.[clxxx] Such accolades came as part of his history-making journey to make 100 Premier League assists, which he accomplished in record time, as it took him just 237 Premier League matches to do so. This beat the previous record held by Cesc Fabregas by over 50 games![clxxxi]

Today, at 32 years of age, De Bruyne shows no real signs of slowing down. The sky is still the limit for this remarkably gifted midfielder, and we can only surmise that he would love to add a few more records to his already impressive list of accolades. For example, De Bruyne would love to track down the all-time PL assist record, which is currently held by Ryan Giggs with 162. Before that, however, he will need to track down the other players with 100+ records, including Frank Lampard (102), Wayne Rooney (103), and Cesc Fabregas (111).[clxxxii] If he can overcome his injuries and stay healthy, it is not hard to believe that he could achieve all this and more.

De Bruyne has even made a believer out of some of the sternest English football pundits who seldom give out praise. This includes Roy Keane and Graeme Souness, who played for Manchester City rivals Manchester United and Liverpool, respectively. The former Red Devil is known to be ultra-critical of players who do not measure up to the standards of his Old Trafford generation. However, Keane has heaped on the praise for De Bruyne. "I love watching him live," the Irishman said. "It's the little details he gets right, in terms of his decision making, weight of pass; he's got a goal in him … He is world-class."[clxxxiii]

De Bruyne's exceptional skills, steady performances, and impressive trophy haul have led many football fans to consider him worthy of winning the Ballon d'Or.[clxxxiv] De Bruyne was named to the third-placed position in the 2022 awards, however, given Manchester City's treble, the Belgian could do even better and take the prestigious award in the future.

Conclusion

Kevin De Bruyne is one of the most famous and well-regarded footballers in the contemporary game and will no doubt continue to be revered for many years to come. While he first came to prominence after his move to Chelsea, he made his name with his various stints in the Bundesliga with Werder Bremen and VfL Wolfsburg.

His move to Manchester City earned him global recognition, as he went on to become one of their elite players within a relatively short period of time. De Bruyne's accomplishments were soon rewarded with trophies and individual awards, none greater than the 2022-23 season when he won the Premier League, the FA Cup, and the UEFA Champions League, affectionately named the treble. And, in addition to his exceptional club career, De Bruyne is considered to be one of the greatest players for the Belgian national team having made close to 100 appearances for them.

Now at 32 years of age and perhaps entering the latter stages of his career, the Belgian phenom shows no significant signs of slowing down. Thus, Kevin De Bruyne may yet add to his many accomplishments and accolades. But regardless, his enduring legacy as one of soccer's greatest midfielders is already etched into the history books and the hearts of football fans around the world.

Final Word/About the Author

Wow! You made it to the end of this book, and you're reading the About the Author section? Now that's impressive and puts you in the top 1% of readers.

Since you're curious about me, I was born and raised in Norwalk, Connecticut. Growing up, I could often be found spending many nights watching basketball, soccer, and football matches with my father in the family living room. I love sports and everything that sports can embody. I believe that sports are one of the most genuine forms of competition, heart, and determination. I write my works to learn more about influential athletes in the hopes that from my writing, you the reader can walk away inspired to put in an equal if not greater amount of hard work and perseverance to pursue your goals.

I've written these stories for over a decade, and loved every moment of it. When I look back on my life, I am most proud of not just having covered so many different athletes' inspirational stories, but for all the times I got e-mails or handwritten letters from readers on the impact my books have had on them.

So thank you from the bottom of my heart for allowing me to do work I find meaningful. I am incredibly grateful for you and your support.

If you're new to my sports biography books, welcome. I have goodies for you as a thank you from me in the pages ahead.

Before we get there though, I have a question for you…

Were you inspired at any point in this book?

If so, would you help someone else get inspired too?

You see, my mission is to inspire sports fans of all ages around the world that anything is possible through hard work and perseverance…but the only way to accomplish this mission is by reaching everyone.

So here's my ask from you:

Most people, regardless of what the saying tells them to do, judge a book by its cover (and its reviews).

If you enjoyed *Kevin De Bruyne: The Inspiring Story of One of Soccer's Star Midfielders*, please help inspire another person needing to hear this story by leaving a review.

Doing so takes less than a minute, and that dose of inspiration can change another person's life in more ways than you can even imagine.

To get that generous 'feel good' feeling and help another person, all you have to do is take 60 seconds and leave a review.

If you're on Audible: hit the three dots in the top right of your device, click rate & review, then leave a few sentences about the book with a star rating.

If you're reading on Kindle or an e-reader: scroll to the bottom of the book, then swipe up and it will prompt a review for you.

If for some reason these have changed: you can head back to Amazon and leave a review right on the book's page.

Thank you for helping another person, and for your support of my writing as an independent author.

Clayton

Like what you read? Then you'll love these too!

This book is one of hundreds of stories I've written. If you enjoyed this story on Kevin De Bruyne, you'll love my other sports biography book series too.

You can find them by visiting my website at claytongeoffreys.com or by scanning the QR code below to follow my author page on Amazon.

Here's a little teaser about each of my sports biography book series:

Soccer Biography Books: This series covers the stories of tennis greats such as Neymar, Harry Kane, Robert Lewandowski, and more.

Basketball Biography Books: This series covers the stories of over 100 NBA greats such as Stephen Curry, LeBron James, Michael Jordan, and more.

Football Biography Books: This series covers the stories of over 50 NFL greats such as Peyton Manning, Tom Brady, and Patrick Mahomes, and more.

Baseball Biography Books: This series covers the stories of over 40 MLB greats such as Aaron Judge, Shohei Ohtani, Mike Trout, and more.

Basketball Leadership Biography Books: This series covers the stories of basketball coaching greats such as Steve Kerr, Gregg Popovich, John Wooden, and more.

Tennis Biography Books: This series covers the stories of tennis greats such as Serena Williams, Rafael Nadal, Andy Roddick, and more.

Women's Basketball Biography Books: This series covers the stories of many WNBA greats such as Diana Taurasi, Sue Bird, Sabrina Ionescu, and more.

Lastly, if you'd like to join my exclusive list where I let you know about my latest books, and gift you free copies of some of my other books, go to **claytongeoffreys.com/goodies**.

Or, if you don't like typing, scan the following QR code here to go there directly. See you there!

Clayton

References

[i] Jackson, Elliot. Kevin De Bruyne labelled a 'complete footballer' as Roy Keane raves about Man City star. The Manchester Evening News. 3 January 2021. Web.

[ii] Redknapp, Jamie. Kevin De Bruyne is world's best midfielder and Man City have treble in their own hands, says Jamie Redknapp. Sky Sports. 30 April 2023. Web.

[iii] Cunningham, Sam. The making of Kevin De Bruyne: From angry red-faced child to England's World Cup nemesis? I News. 15 June 2018. Web.

[iv] Edwards, John. MADE IN BELGIUM: WHAT WE LEARNED ABOUT KEVIN DE BRUYNE. Manchester City. 11 September 2020. Web.

[v] De Bruyne, Kevin. Let Me Talk. The Player's Tribune. 15 April 2019. Web.

[vi] Harris, Nick. Kevin De Bruyne's first taste of stardom was for his exemplary attendance at school... but now he's preparing for the big time as he closes in on a move to Manchester City. The Daily Mail. 29 August 2015. Web.

[vii] Turk, Alex. Man City star Kevin De Bruyne grew up on oil money and may have played for African country. The Express. 5 April 2023. Web.

[viii] Harraz, Marwan. Watch: De Bruyne stuns interviewer as Man City star picks Michael Owen as his favourite player growing up. GOAL. 12 February 2022. Web.

[ix] Orme, Daniel. Kevin De Bruyne admitted he was a Liverpool fan and named ex-Reds star he idolised. The Mirror. 2 July 2023. Web.

[x] Hampson, Andy. Kevin De Bruyne forced to use left foot as a child – to protect friend's flowers. Breaking News Ireland. 12 May 2022. Web.

[xi] Let's Engage. Kevin De Bruyne. Let's Engage. 2023. Web.

[xii] Blackburn, Martin. BRUY DONE GOOD De Bruyne reveals rejection from foster family as kid spurred him on to be Man City superstar. The Sun. 15 April 2019. Web.

[xiii] ESPN. Burnley's Steven Defour not surprised by Kevin De Bruyne's rise. ESPN. 21 October 2017. Web.

[xiv] Smeets, Rudi. De Bruyne may be out for months with glandular fever. Nieuwsblad. 21 October 2010. Web. [Translated].

[xv] De Morgen. Kevin De Bruyne sidelined for four to six weeks. De Morgen. 8 August 2011. Web.

[xvi] TNT Sports. Kevin De Bruyne of Genk vows to pile on the misery for Chelsea. The Guardian. 31 October 2011. Web.

[xvii] Sporza. WATCH: 10 years ago: Kevin De Bruyne rolls over Club Brugge

with 3 goals. Sporza. 19 October 2021. Web. [Translated].

xviii Hattenstone, Simon. 'After a while it eats you up': Kevin De Bruyne on dealing with the spotlight, life at home and whether he gets paid too much. The Guardian. 26 November 2022. Web.

xix Fifield, Dominic. Chelsea sign midfielder Kevin De Bruyne from Genk on five-year deal. The Guardian. 31 January 2012. Web.

xx HLN. Eight years ago, Kevin De Bruyne experienced a minor farewell at RC Genk: "I immediately knew it was bad". HLN.Be. 27 April 2020. Web. [Translated].

xxi Pilger, Sam. The Making of a Magician: How Kevin De Bruyne Became One of the World's Best. Bleacher Report. 10 May 2018. Web.

xxii Cummings, Michael. Seattle Sounders vs. Chelsea: 6 Things We Learned from Preseason Friendly. Bleacher Report. 19 July 2012. Web.

xxiii Parker, Graham. MLS All Stars 3-2 Chelsea. The Guardian. 26 July 2012. Web.

xxiv Hynter, David. Chelsea's Kevin De Bruyne joins Werder Bremen on season-long loan. The Guardian. 31 July 2012. Web.

xxv The Daily Mail. Chelsea send £7m youngster De Bruyne to Werder Bremen on season-long loan. The Daily Mail. 2 August 2012. Web.

xxvi Jiang, Allan. Chelsea FC: Kevin De Bruyne Loan Report vs. Borussia Dortmund. Bleacher Report. 25 August 2012. Web.

xxvii Weser Kurier. First Werder goal for Kevin de Bruyne. Weser Kurier. 15 September 2012. Web. [Translated].

xxviii Winter, Sebastian. Watschn for Werder. Spiegel Sports. 23 February 2013. Web. [Translated].

xxix Werder Bremen. DE BRUYNE COMMITS TO WERDER. Werder Bremen. 18 October 2012. Web.

xxx Bundesliga. De Bruyne: 'Just happy to be safe'. Bundesliga. May 2013. Web.

xxxi Houten, Declan. The Best Moments of Kevin De Bruyne's Career So Far. 90 Min. 28 June 2020. Web.

xxxii Jenas, Jermaine. Man City: Kevin de Bruyne's drive is what sets him apart - Jermaine Jenas. BBC Sport. 5 April 2018. Web.

xxxiii BBC Sport. Kevin de Bruyne: Wolfsburg sign Chelsea midfielder. BBC. 18 January 2014. Web.

xxxiv The Guardian. Chelsea sell Kevin De Bruyne to Wolfsburg. The Guardian. 18 January 2014. Web.

xxxv Ladyman, Ian. Kevin De Bruyne exclusive interview - the 10 best quotes: 'I have no problem with Jose Mourinho but I think Chelsea had a different view of me than I had'. The Daily Mail. 24 October 2016. Web.

xxxvi Askew, Joshua. Case Study: Wolfsburg 4-1 Bayern Munich 30/1/2015. Holding Midfield. 8 February 2015. Web.

xxxvii Singer, Jonny. Wolfsburg 3-1 Inter Milan: Naldo and Kevin de Bruyne double earn Germans a lead after Rodrigo Palacio's away goal. The Daily Mail. 12 March 2015. Web.

xxxviii Stuttgarter Zeitung. De Bruyne turns the game around. Stuttgarter Zeitung. 12 March 2015. Web.

xxxix Saville, Jack. Kevin De Bruyne: The Wolfsburg match that made Man City sign him for £55m. Give Me Sport. 15 April 2021. Web.

xl Holsbeek, Florian. Pierre Denier is impressed: "De Bruyne is ready for the European top". Walfoot. 13 March 2015. Web. [Translated].

xli Adams, Tom. Kevin De Bruyne exclusive: I can't promise I will stay at Wolfsburg. TNT Sports. 13 May 2015. Web.

xlii Cischinsky, Yannick. DE BRUYNE: WERDER IS GOING THROUGH "GOOD DEVELOPMENT". Werder Bremen. 26 February 2015. Web.

xliii Bienkowski, Stefan. Kevin De Bruyne Magic Ensures Wolfsburg Victory over Dortmund in DFB-Pokal. Bleacher Report. 30 May 2015. Web.

xliv DFB. DE BRUYNE: THE MAN BEHIND THE SUPERSTAR. DFB. 2015. Web.

xlv UEFA. De Bruyne named player of the year in Germany. UEFA. 26 July 2015. Web.

xlvi Campo, Carlo. Kevin De Bruyne sets Bundesliga record for assists in a single season. The Score. 16 May 2015. Web.

xlvii Bairner, Robin. Bayern Munich's Muller surpasses De Bruyne to set new Bundesliga assists record. GOAL. 27 June 2020. Web.

xlviii Bundesliga. De Bruyne voted 2014/15 Player of the Season. Bundesliga. May 2015. Web.

xlix Bundesliga. On-song De Bruyne new leader of the Wolfpack. Bundesliga. 2014. Web.

l Sport1. De Bruyne voted cup hero. Sport1. June 2015. Web.

li Bundesliga. Kevin De Bruyne: Manchester City's majestic midfielder, made in the Bundesliga. Bundesliga. 2022. Web.

lii The Irish Independent. Boss is fed up with De Bruyne rumours. The Irish Independent. 15 August 2015. Web.

liii Ullal, Naveen. Manchester United target Kevin De Bruyne urged to continue at Wolfsburg by manager Dieter Hecking. IB Times. 3 December 2015. Web.

liv BBC Sport. Kevin De Bruyne: Manchester City sign Wolfsburg midfielder. BBC. 30 August 2015. Web.

lv Goddard, Nicholas. Kevin De Bruyne can reach Lionel Messi and

Cristiano Ronaldo's level, claims his first Belgium boss Georges Leekens. The Daily Mail. 10 September 2015. Web.

lvi ESPN. Kevin De Bruyne should develop at Wolfsburg before big move – Wilmots. ESPN. 18 February 2015. Web.

lvii Melzer, Dennis. OH LORD! VFL WOLFSBURG DEFEATED FC BAYERN IN THE SUPERCUP ON PENALTIES. Eurosport. 2 August 2015. Web.

lviii The Guardian. Manchester City confirm signing of Kevin De Bruyne from Wolfsburg. The Guardian. 30 August 2015. Web.

lix Manchester City. DE BRUYNE AND HART PAY TRIBUTE TO GOAL-KING KUN. Manchester City. 3 October 2015. Web. Web.

lx Taylor, Daniel. Manchester City's derby delight as De Bruyne inspires win over United. The Guardian. 10 September 2016. Web.

lxi Mumford, Jack. DE BRUYNE: WE FOUGHT UNTIL THE END! Manchester City. 10 September 2016. Web.

lxii Boyle, Robyn. Footballer Kevin De Bruyne is Sportsman of the Year in Belgium. The Bulletin. 20 December 2015. Web.

lxiii Ashenden, Mark. Manchester City's Kevin De Bruyne faces six weeks out, say representatives. Sky Sports. 28 January 2016. Web.

lxiv Aarons, Ed. Manchester City's Kevin De Bruyne out for 10 weeks due to knee injury. The Guardian. 28 January 2016. Web.

lxv Morgan, Richard. Bournemouth 0-4 Manchester City: Returning Kevin De Bruyne keeps Blues in fourth. Sky Sports. 9 April 2016. Web.

lxvi Taylor, Daniel. Kevin De Bruyne kills off PSG and fires Manchester City into semi-finals. The Guardian. 12 April 2016. Web.

lxvii Barnard, Sam. De Bruyne screamer seals Man City's seat in semi-finals at expense of poor PSG. Coral. 13 April 2016. Web.

lxviii Keble, Alex. Kevin De Bruyne Comments on Chelsea Exit, Jose Mourinho, Pep Guardiola and More. Bleacher Report. 3 November 2016. Web.

lxix Booth, Mark. ARSENAL EDGE FIVE-GOAL THRILLER IN SWEDEN. Manchester City. 7 August 2016. Web.

lxx Blackburn, Martin. KDB FEARS MONTH OUT Kevin de Bruyne faces missing at least three weeks with hamstring injury as Manchester City attacker flies to Barcelona for tests. The Sun. 25 September 2016. Web.

lxxi Goncalves, Renato. WATCH: Kevin De Bruyne scores beautiful free-kick as Manchester City stun Barcelona. Biiter & Blue. 1 November 2016. Web.

lxxii De Bruyne, Kevin. CITY V BARCA: DE BRUYNE REACTION. Manchester City FC TV. 1 November 2016. Video.

lxxiii Pollard, Rob. GUARDIOLA: DE BRUYNE TO MISS DERBY

SHOWDOWN. Manchester City. 25 October 2016. Web.

lxxiv Surlis, Patrick. Monaco 3-1 Man City (Agg: 6-6): City out of Champions League on away goals. Sky Sports. 16 March 2016. Web

lxxv Bonn, Kyle. No Champions League away goals rule in 2023: What happens if teams are tied on aggregate goals after second leg? The Sporting News. 17 May 2023. Web.

lxxvi Edwards, Luke. Kevin De Bruyne: My row with David Silva was like arguing with my wife. The Telegraph. 18 October 2017. Web.

lxxvii Pitt-Brooke, Jack. Pep Guardiola hails Kevin De Bruyne as 'one of the best players' he has ever seen after Manchester City's win. The Independent. 13 September 2017. Web.

lxxviii Reuters. Kevin De Bruyne performance leaves Pep Guardiola speechless. TNT Sports. 16 December 2017. Web.

lxxix Handler, Paul. AGUERO GOALS AND CAPTAIN KDB: TALKING POINTS. Manchester City. 10 January 2018. Web.

lxxx Taylor, Daniel. West Brom stun Manchester United to hand Manchester City the title. The Guardian. 15 April 2018. Web.

lxxxi Banks, Marcus. Centurions: The Manchester City team that surpassed Arsenal's Invincibles. Manchester Evening News. 19 November 2019. Web.

lxxxii Burt, Jason. Kevin De Bruyne could be out for four months after suffering freak knee injury in training. The Telegraph. 15 August 2018. Web.

lxxxiii O'Callaghan, Rory. Kevin De Bruyne out for 'two to four months' after suffering knee injury in Manchester City training. Sky Sports. 16 August 2018. Web.

lxxxiv Marsden, Rory. Kevin De Bruyne Reportedly Set to Return from Injury for Man City vs. Burnley. Bleacher Report. 8 October 2018. Web.

lxxxv Bennett, Tom. Football news - Kevin de Bruyne returns from injury ahead of schedule to start against Shakhtar. TNT Sports. 23 October 2018. Web.

lxxxvi Jackson, Jackson. Kevin De Bruyne's injury mars Manchester City's stroll past Fulham. The Guardian. 1 November 2018. Web.

lxxxvii Manchester City. GUARDIOLA PROVIDES UPDATE ON DE BRUYNE. Manchester City. 30 December 2018. Web.

lxxxviii Bezants, Jack. Angry Kevin De Bruyne 'stormed down the tunnel' after being taken off during Manchester City's Carabao Cup thrashing of Burton. The Daily Mail. 11 January 2019. Web.

lxxxix Critchley, Mark. Kevin De Bruyne injury: Manchester City midfielder ruled out of derby against United. The Independent. 23 April 2019. Web.

xc Pollard, Rob. MANCHESTER CITY WIN PREMIER LEAGUE TITLE. Manchester City. 12 May 2019. Web.

[xci] Manchester City. DE BRUYNE: I THOUGHT MY SEASON WAS DONE. Manchester City. 12 May 2019. Web.

[xcii] Jolly, Richard. Pep Guardiola hits out at VAR after Llorente's disputed goal for Spurs. The Guardian. 18 April 2019. Web.

[xciii] Peach, Simon. Kevin de Bruyne keen to take time to appreciate Manchester City's staggering season of success. The Independent. 19 May 2019. Web.

[xciv] Pollard, Rob. CITY END ASIA TOUR WITH FINE YOKOHAMA WIN. Manchester City. 27 July 2019. Web.

[xcv] The Metro. Kevin De Bruyne a doubt for Manchester City's clash with Wolves due to ankle injury. The Metro. 15 November 2019. Web.

[xcvi] Sadhanand, Srinivas. Kevin De Bruyne names his best-ever performance in a Man City shirt, not against Wolves. Manchester City News. 26 April 2023. Web.

[xcvii] Jackson, Jamie. Kevin De Bruyne to have test on injured shoulder before derby at Old Trafford. The Guardian. 6 March 2020. Web.

[xcviii] Conn, David. English football's shutdown until April means season may never be completed. The Guardian. 13 March 2020. Web.

[xcix] MacInnes, Paul. Premier League returns in new guise after overcoming Covid-19 challenges. The Guardian. 16 June 2020. Web.

[c] Sky Sports. Kevin De Bruyne wins Premier League Player of the Season. Sky Sports. 16 August 2020. Web

[ci] Cormack, James. The most assists in a single Premier League season. 90 Min. 25 October 2022. Web.

[cii] The Athletic. Kevin De Bruyne out for up to six weeks with hamstring injury. The Athletic. 21 January 2021. Web.

[ciii] Jackson, Jamie. 'Irreplaceable' Kevin De Bruyne out for up to six weeks for Manchester City. The Guardian. 22 January 2021. Web.

[civ] Pollard, Rob. MANCHESTER CITY CROWNED 2020-21 PREMIER LEAGUE CHAMPIONS. Manchester City. 11 May 2021. Web.

[cv] Brennan, Stuart. Kevin De Bruyne speaks out on his Champions League final nightmare with Man City. Manchester Evening News. 18 October 2021. Web.

[cvi] Hunter, Andy. De Bruyne insists his career will not be defined by Champions League final. The Guardian. 5 June 2023. Web.

[cvii] Johnson, Isaac. Sergio Aguero details why Man City star Kevin De Bruyne is world class. Manchester Evening News. 4 May 2022. Web.

[cviii] GOAL. De Bruyne admits playing striker was 'bizarre' after Man City win against Chelsea. GOAL. 3 January 2021. Web.

[cix] Sansom, Dan. Kevin De Bruyne: Pep Guardiola says Man City midfielder

a doubt for Norwich game due to ankle injury. Sky Sports. 20 August 2021. Web.

cx The Guardian. Manchester City's Kevin De Bruyne isolating after positive Covid test. The Guardian. 19 November 2021. Web.

cxi Jackson, Jamie. Kevin De Bruyne admits his body is still recovering from Covid-19 and injuries. The Guardian. 15 December 2021. Web.

cxii Clayton, David. CITY EDGE SEVEN-GOAL THRILLER IN CHAMPIONS LEAGUE CLASSIC. Manchester City. 26 April 2022. Web.

cxiii ESPN. Kevin De Bruyne scores four as Manchester City restore Premier League lead. ESPN. 17 May 2023. Web.

cxiv James, Stuart. Best Premier League performances: No 22, Kevin De Bruyne for Man City v Wolves. The Athletic. 12 July 2022. Web.

cxv McNulty, Phil. Manchester City 3-2 Aston Villa 2. BBC Sport. 22 May 2022. Web.

cxvi Leigh, Neil. CITY STAGE STUNNING VILLA FIGHTBACK TO RETAIN PREMIER LEAGUE CROWN. Manchester City. 22 May 2022. Web.

cxvii McDonnell, David. Inside Man City's trophy parade: Kevin De Bruyne drunk and Pep Guardiola dancing. The Mirror. 23 May 2022. Web.

cxviii Mumford, Jack. KEVIN DE BRUYNE'S ASSISTS RECORD: SEASON BY SEASON. Manchester City. 2023. Web.

cxix Edwards, John. CITY COMPLETE HAALAND TRANSFER. Manchester City. 13 June 2022. Web.

cxx Keighley, Freddie. Arsenal target Gabriel Jesus sent message by Kevin De Bruyne after transfer talks held. The Mirror. 3 May 2022. Web.

cxxi Jackson, Kieran. Kevin De Bruyne on Man City teammate Raheem Sterling: 'I thought he would be a bit of a dickhead'. The Independent. 15 April 2019. Web.

cxxii Manchester City. DE BRUYNE: THIS IS THE REAL RAHEEM! Manchester City. 16 April 2019. Web.

cxxiii Sidle, Ryan. Kevin de Bruyne has been voted as the best midfielder in Premier League history. Sport Bible. 30 December 2022. Web.

cxxiv Percival, Holly. DE BRUYNE: HOPEFULLY WE CAN MAKE THE SEASON EVEN BETTER! Manchester City. 3 June 2023. Web.

cxxv Pollard, Rob. MANCHESTER CITY WIN THIRD SUCCESSIVE PREMIER LEAGUE TITLE. Manchester City. 20 May 2023. Web.

cxxvi Benge, James. RB Leipzig vs. Manchester City: Illness rules Kevin De Bruyne out of Champions League trip. CBS Sports. 21 February 2023. Web.

cxxvii Dunbar, Graham. De Bruyne again goes off injured in Champions League final but Man City finds a way without him. AP News. 10 June 2023.

Web.

cxxviii Blackburn, Martin. THE WIFES ALWAYS RIGHT Kevin de Bruyne says it's a 'shame' as he is forced to admit his wife was right after Man City's historic treble win. The Sun. 11 June 2023. Web.

cxxix Hynter, David. Kevin De Bruyne savours sweat and sacrifice as treble dream comes true. The Guardian. 11 June 2023. Web.

cxxx Elliot, Ed. Man City players 'drank all the alcohol in Manchester' celebrating Premier League title. The Independent. 25 May 2023. Web.

cxxxi Mayo, Marco. Kevin De Bruyne's dancing and Jack Grealish doused in champagne: The best Man City parade pictures. The Standard. 13 June 2023. Web.

cxxxii Bray, Joe. Erling Haaland explains key to Kevin De Bruyne partnership at Man City. Manchester Evening News. 1 December 2022. Web.

cxxxiii Schofield, Will. 13 players who could've played for obscure national teams - like De Bruyne and Gullit. The Daily Star. 15 May 2023. Web.

cxxxiv Robson, James. Man City star De Bruyne is smiling again, says Wilmots. Manchester Evening News. 26 June 2016. Web.

cxxxv Abbandonato, Paul. Wales 3-1 Belgium match report: Brilliant Wales thrash Belgians to roar into semi-finals of Euro 2016. Wales Online. 1 July 2016. Web.

cxxxvi Howard, Derren. KEV DE BLAMER Euro 2016: Kevin De Bruyne slams Belgium boss Marc Wilmots after shock exit to Wales. The Sun. 2 July 2016. Web.

cxxxvii ITV. Wilmots: De Bruyne playing with smile on his face. ITV. 25 June

cxxxviii The Guardian. Roberto Martínez appointed as new Belgium head coach. The Guardian. 3 August 2016. Web.

cxxxix Liew, Jonathan. World Cup 2018: Belgium's Roberto Martinez gamble pays off as big-name players start pulling in same direction. The Independent. 7 July 2018. Web.

cxl Sky Sports. Kevin De Bruyne hits out at Roberto Martinez over Belgium tactics. Sky Sports. 14 November 2017. Web.

cxli Sky Sports. Kevin De Bruyne says current Belgium team are 'calmer' than ever. Sky Sports. 25 June 2018. Web.

cxlii Ladner, Ben. World Cup 2018: Advancing Scenarios For Each Group. Sports Illustrated. 24 June 2018. Web.

cxliii Kelner, Martha. Defeating England is not a priority for Belgium, says Roberto Martínez. The Guardian. 27 June 2018. Web.

cxliv Burnton, Simon. Belgium 3-2 Japan: World Cup 2018 – as it happened. The Guardian. 2 July 2018. Web.

cxlv Hampson, Andy. Kevin De Bruyne: Belgium proved World Cup credentials to beat Brazil. The Irish Independent. 6 July 2018. Web.

cxlvi Kappel, David. FIFA Announce Official Team Of The 2018 FIFA World Cup. SNL24. 18 July 2018. Web.

cxlvii Sky Sports. Kevin De Bruyne: Belgium midfielder set to miss Euro 2020 opener against Russia, says Roberto Martinez. Sky Sports. 5 June 2021. Web.

cxlviii Bairner, Robin. De Bruyne limps out of Belgium's Euro 2020 clash with Portugal. GOAL. 27 June 2021. Web.

cxlix Walker-Roberts, James. Football news - Kevin De Bruyne admits regret over painkillers, says he was concussed in Champions League final. TNT Sports. 6 October 2021. Web.

cl Latham Coyle, Harry. 'It is a little bit boring' - Kevin De Bruyne admits repeated Wales games have become tedious. TNT Sports. 22 September 2022. Web.

cli Chiu, Nigel. World Cup 2022: 'We're too old' – Kevin De Bruyne says Belgium have 'no chance' of winning in Qatar. TNT Sports. 26 November 2022. Web.

clii Bishop, Adrian. 'I think our chance was 2018': Kevin De Bruyne writes off Belgium's World Cup hopes as the Man City talisman says their golden generation is 'ageing' and has 'lost some key players' after finishing third in Russia. The Daily Mail. 26 November 2022. Web.

cliii TNT Sports. How is Man of the Match awarded at the 2022 World Cup in Qatar? How does the voting work? TNT Sports. 25 November 2022. Web.

cliv Mullock, Simon. Kevin De Bruyne's 'erratic behaviour' blamed for Belgium's World Cup nightmare. The Mirror. 28 November 2022. Web.

clv Walker, Ron. Roberto Martinez leaves role as Belgium manager after World Cup group-stage exit. Sky Sports. 2 December 2022. Web.

clvi SPORTSMAX. Germany 2-3 Belgium: De Bruyne dazzles as Tedesco era offers promise. SPORTSMAX. 28 March 2023. Web.

clvii McGrath, Mike. Exclusive Kevin De Bruyne interview: 'Being an introvert is not always easy, but on the pitch I am a different person'. The Telegraph. 6 December 2019. Web.

clviii Marsh, Jonny. KEVIN CARBONARA Kevin De Bruyne has his own secret low-fat Kevin Carbonara sauce – and like Tyson Fury, plenty of Premier League footballers have the same meal before every game. The Sun. 12 December 2018. Web.

clix Manchester City. TASTE TACTICS WITH KEVIN DE BRUYNE. Manchester City. 30 June 2022. Web.

clx Malata, Chisanga. SHOTS ON TARGET Man City star Kevin De Bruyne 'gets wasted' on shots on holiday after soaking up sun on yacht in Ibiza. The

Sun. 4 July 2022. Web.
clxi Aizlewood, Josh. Kevin De Bruyne on eating with Julius Caesar, listening to Post Malone and Japanese dining in Las Vegas. The Times. 2 October 2022. Web.
clxii Terreur, Kristof. Kevin De Bruyne: the stubborn boy who developed into a world beater. The Guardian. 20 October 2017. Web.
clxiii Gaughan, Jack. Even Kevin De Bruyne's family have succumbed to Erling Haaland-mania with his son sporting the Norwegian's famous haircut... as the talented midfielder wonders if Man City aren't becoming TOO accustomed to success. The Daily Mail. 8 June 2023. Web.
clxiv Manchester City. DE BRUYNE'S FAVOURITE CITY KIT AND GO-TO VIDEO GAME. Manchester City. 5 March 2020. Web.
clxv Wright, Chris. Manchester City's Kevin De Bruyne is a big Bake Off fan. ESPN. 12 October 2015. Web.
clxvi Corking, Graham. MANCHESTER CITY'S KEVIN DE BRUYNE HAS A RATHER SURPRISING HOBBY. Here is the City. 12 October 2015. Web.
clxvii Walker, Thomas. Belgian Midfielder Kevin De Bruyne's Cars. Carmoola. 20 October 2022. Web.
clxviii Moxon, Daniel. Christian Horner tells Kevin De Bruyne how he can land F1 drive with Red Bull. The Mirror. 1 September 2022. Web.
clxix UEFA. De Bruyne offers support to Special Olympics. UEFA. 30 September 2014. Web.
clxx Kidd, Robert. Manchester City's Kevin De Bruyne: 'I Understand What My Body And Mind Want'. Forbes. 29 July 2022. Web.
clxxi Manchester City. DE BRUYNE PLAYS PART IN COVID-19 RELIEF FUND-RAISING DRIVE. Manchester City. 21 April 2020. Web.
clxxii Dawson, Robert. Man City seek signing to replace injured De Bruyne – Guardiola. ESPN. 18 August 2023. Web.
clxxiii Bradley, Ciaran. Man City seek signing to replace injured De Bruyne – Guardiola. Off the Ball. 2020. Web.
clxxiv The Hard Tackle. Kevin De Bruyne uninterested in Manchester City exit. The Hard Tackle. 10 September 2023. Web.
clxxv Menzies, John. Kevin De Bruyne wanted by Atletico Madrid. Football Espana. 1 January 2023. Web.
clxxvi Johnson, Isaac. Pep Guardiola statue claim made as Man City ace Kevin De Bruyne told why he could follow. Manchester Evening News. 1 June 2023. Web.
clxxvii BBC Sport. Man City v Real Madrid: 'Kevin de Bruyne still needs his legacy moment'. BBC. 17 May 2023. Web.

clxxviii City Xtra. "IT DEPENDS WHO YOU ASK!" – KEVIN DE BRUYNE HITS BACK AT LEGACY-DEFINING CHAMPIONS LEAGUE FINAL NOTION. One Football. 6 June 2023. Web.

clxxix Brown, Luke. Kevin de Bruyne can become as good as Lionel Messi and Cristiano Ronaldo, says Roberto Martinez. The Independent. 9 November 2017. Web.

clxxx Prenn, Tamara. Kevin De Bruyne is crowned the best Premier League midfielder of ALL-TIME by voters - narrowly topping the list ahead of Steven Gerrard, Frank Lampard and Paul Scholes... but which other current player makes the top 10? The Daily Mail. 13 April 2023. Web.

clxxxi Prenn, Tamara. Kevin De Bruyne is the FASTEST player in Premier League history to reach 100 assists, edging out a former Arsenal and two Manchester United legends... as fans hail Man City star as 'the best midfielder to EVER grace this league'. The Daily Mail. 8 April 2023. Web.

clxxxii Mendola, Nicholas. Premier League all-time assist leaders: Mohamed Salah moves into Top 20. NBC Sports. 11 November 2023. Web.

clxxxiii All Football. Roy Keane stuns Laura Woods by describing De Bruyne's performance as 'sexy'. All Football. 1 March 2023. Web.

clxxxiv TNT Sports. Ballon d'Or 2023: Who can stop favourite Lionel Messi from winning an eighth trophy? What are the latest odds? TNT Sports. 20 October 2023. Web.

Printed in Dunstable, United Kingdom